Saying Goodbye

Saying
Goodbye

to the people, places, and things
in our lives

Julie Rember *Editor*
Mike O'Mary *Series Editor*

Dream of Things
Downers Grove Illinois USA

Saying Goodbye
Editor: Julie Rember
Series Editor: Mike O'Mary

Published by Dream of Things
Downers Grove, Illinois USA
dreamofthings.com

Saying goodbye : to the people, places, and things in our lives /
Julie Rember, editor ; Mike O'Mary, series editor.
    p. cm.
    "Dream of things anthologies"
    ISBN 9780982579442

1. Grief. 2. Bereavement. 3. Death--Collected works. 3. Attitude to death --Collected works. 4. Death--Psychological aspects. 5. Loss (Psychology). 6. Adult children of aging parents--Family relationships. I. Rember, Julie. II. O'Mary, Mike. III. Title.

BF789.D4 S29 2010
155.9/37—dc22
2010936283

Dream of Things provides discounts to educators, book clubs, writers groups, and others. Contact customerservice@dreamofthings.com or call 847-321-1390.

Cover design: Megan Kearney
Interior design: Susan Veach

First Dream of Things edition

Contents

Foreword

hen my daughter was five, her great-grandfather died. At the funeral, I read a story about him, and his two sons-in-law each said a few heartfelt words.

After the last person spoke, my daughter, who was sitting in the front row next to her grandmother, stood up in her chair, turned around to face the room full of mourners, and said, "Is that it?"

That moment sticks with me because it shows that in the midst of the most solemn of goodbyes, there is sadness, yes. But there is also irony and humor and in some strange way, a sense of continuity. So it is, I believe, with all goodbyes.

Years later, Stephen Parrish, author of *The Tavernier Stones*, sent me a story called "Bridget." I had just launched Dream of Things with the intent of publishing anthologies of creative nonfiction that will fill the gap between popular anthologies that publish stories I regard as "short and sweet" (sometimes so saccharine-sweet they are hard to

1

swallow), and the *Best American Essays* series, which I love, but which tend to be quite a bit longer. So the goal for Dream of Things anthologies is to be not short and sweet, but short and *deep*. With depth comes authenticity. The result is stories that are easier to swallow because they are authentic, and easier to digest because they average 1,250 words in length.

Stephen Parrish's story fit the bill...short and deep...but it didn't fit neatly into any of the anthology topics that were in the works. So we created a new anthology—a collection of stories about saying goodbye. The topic struck a chord, and the stories came pouring in from around the world... from the United States, Canada, Ireland, Great Britain, France, Italy, Germany, Australia, New Zealand, and elsewhere. The result is this book—a remarkable collection of stories, and the first of what I hope will be many anthologies from Dream of Things.

I say these stories are remarkable not just because of the quality of the writing and the subject matter, but also because a remarkable thing happened as I read them. I cried at sad stories and laughed at funny ones...that was no surprise. But I also learned valuable lessons about how people say goodbye—sometimes under the most difficult of circumstances. I learned because the authors who contributed to this collection were unflinchingly open and honest when it came to sharing very personal stories about how they and their loved ones say goodbye. It was a lesson that has better prepared me for whatever the future may hold. Thanks to the authors and their beautiful stories about saying goodbye to family members, relationships, jobs, pets, old homes, couches, jogging suits, the past, and other things, I will be better at saying goodbye in my life whenever the time comes. You will be, too.

I hope you enjoy these stories. Goodbye—for now.

Mike O'Mary, *Series Editor*

Introduction

In a language containing a quarter of a million words, we can say the same thing many ways—farewell, see ya, bye-bye, catch you later, ta-ta, goodbye. We even borrow words from other languages: adios, adieu, hasta la vista, ciao. On the other hand, just one word—*goodbye*—can mean many things. We use it when we head out on a fifteen-minute walk around the block, or after we've spent an evening with good friends. But we also say it when we lose something forever—a friendship, a home, a loved one, an idea of ourselves.

And often, we can't say "hello" again until we've said "goodbye."

Last year, I helped my mother with a book project. She was compiling the letters that my grandfather wrote to my grandmother when he was stationed in the South Pacific during World War II. Reading letters I hadn't even known existed, I met a man who had hopes for the future, questions about his place in the world and universe, ambitions for his family and himself—not to mention a terrific sense of humor.

I thought back to the last time I saw my grandfather alive, back in 1993, after he had descended into the darkness of dementia. Back then, his death came as a relief. His memorial service remembered someone far different than the childlike person my grandpa had become.

Now, having read the letters he wrote to his wife when he was twenty-nine, in the midst of great fear and danger and longing, I wish I could say both "hello" and "goodbye" to the grandfather I never really knew. For the first time, I truly grieve for him.

The stories in *Saying Goodbye* explore how we leave the people, places, and things in our lives. In "The Evolution of Your Goodbyes," Ruth Schiffmann painfully and beautifully shares her response to her father's decline. Dianna Calareso's "We Are Gathered," a meditation on family, grief, and hope, weaves together the deaths of her brother, cousin, and grandfather with the joy of a wedding. And Diana M. Amadeo and Katrin Horowitz both tell stories of how women close to them faced death with courage and dignity.

Not all of these stories are about saying goodbye to someone who is dying. Glynis Scrivens uses her son's "Santa sack" as a metaphor for his crossing over the threshold between childhood and adulthood. Saying goodbye to teaching after thirty-seven years isn't easy for Ann Ingalls, but her description evokes both the joy and heartbreak of leaving one stage of life for another.

Other stories in this collection describe losing a pet, leaving behind a child's pacifier, letting go of the anger and pain of old enmities, even the agony of giving up a newborn for adoption.

Saying goodbye isn't always a bad thing. Annmarie B. Tait's account of her family's sofas will leave you in stitches. And by the end of "Au Revoir May" by Jane Shortall, you'll feel like cheering.

Taken together, these thirty-one stories serve as amazing examples of people saying heartfelt goodbyes with grace, dignity, and good humor. I am grateful to the authors who shared them, and I hope this book will spark conversations about all the ways we say goodbye.

Julie Rember, *Editor*

Bridget

Stephen Parrish

t was February, 1967. I was eight years old. My family had just moved from Kentucky to a small town on the Vermilion River in Illinois. A Catholic grade school was within walking distance of our new house, so my parents took advantage of an opportunity to reverse a heathen trend and enrolled me.

The first thing I learned when I joined my third grade class was one of my fellow students, a girl named Bridget, couldn't meet me yet because she was in the hospital. Not long afterwards, Bridget died.

If my teacher, Sister Joseph, had known that what she was about to do would traumatize me, I'm sure she wouldn't have done it. She took the class for a walk. We marched down the street in the morning chill, turned a corner, and entered a funeral home. On display in the middle of a large and otherwise empty room was a casket. The casket was open, and there lay Bridget.

Sister Joseph instructed us to gather next to the casket on our knees, press our palms together, and recite a sequence of exhortations on behalf of Bridget's soul. As luck or providence would have it, I ended up kneeling next to Bridget's face, my elbows resting on the edge of the casket. Students jostling for position behind me shoved me even farther forward, so that I was leaning over her.

She didn't look at all dead. She looked like she was asleep. She wore a white lace dress, and her hands were clasped across her stomach. She had soft brown hair, smooth skin, and long eyelashes. She was pretty.

We said prayers. We sang songs. All the while I stared into Bridget's face, from fourteen inches away, waiting for her eyes to flutter open. Waiting for her to look up at the strange kid gazing down at her. The only kid in the class she didn't know. The only third grade classmate whose acquaintance she would make *after* she died.

On the way back to school, in an effort to grab onto something corporeal, something of existential certainty, I searched the sidewalk beneath my feet. I was ready to pick up a flower, if one should happen to appear so early in the year, or a frog; anything I understood, anything I could hold onto that reconnected me with a world in which one sunrise followed another, and no sunrise was ever the last.

I saw a penny. I broke ranks to snatch it up. It shined with freshly minted newness. 1966, it said. The last full year of Bridget's life.

The church held a memorial service. I attended, at Sister Joseph's insistence, and not knowing where else to sit, I joined a group dressed all in black, clustered near the front. I realized too late it was Bridget's family. No one complained about an innocent-looking, towheaded, eight-year-old intruder, so I stayed put.

The priest spoke in a plastic and authoritative tone. He asked a rhetorical question, one distinguished by the absence of a question mark, of a rational follow-up, of even an attempt. One whose answer eluded him as much as anyone:

Why did Bridget die.

Sitting to my right was a man I guessed was Bridget's grandfather. His eyebrows were in bushy disarray, the way older men who no longer fussed with their appearance let them grow. He was convulsing. Holding the backrest of the pew in front of him for support. Gasping for air between stifled sobs.

He didn't know why Bridget died, either.

I went home after the service and did the only thing an eight-year-old could do, one whose newest friend was dead, and dead on the day he met her: I made her my imaginary companion.

For a girl, Bridget was pretty good at climbing trees. And wading in creeks. She clutched her white dress above her knees to keep it dry, and was careful not to slip on rocks. She didn't like toy soldiers or G.I. Joes, but she understood when I wanted to play with them. And with other kids. She never got in the way.

I told my dad about her. I told him I had an invisible

companion, and that she was a girl. What he said was in-sightful: "Enjoy her while she's still around."

As I got older, and flesh-and-blood girls took part in my life in a way an imaginary one couldn't, Bridget's white shoes and stockings remained disconcertingly visible beneath a curtain that had already begun to separate us. She hadn't grown at all since we met at the funeral home. She was still eight. I needed to be with kids my own age. It was time to tell her.

You have to go now, Bridget. You can't keep waiting for me.

The girl disappeared but the curtain remained. Behind it were memories of running through sprinklers and chasing after lightning bugs, all stored away like monochrome prints in an old attic. As the years passed I sometimes watched the curtain, hoping to see movement, but nobody was back there. I eventually came to realize that I hadn't let Bridget go after all.

In 2005, thirty-eight years after she died, I kept a prom-ise I'd made when my family moved away from that small town on the Vermilion River. I had business in northern Il-linois, and when it was concluded I aimed my rental car south, navigated back to my boyhood home, and found my way to the library.

It was easier than I expected. The librarian showed me how to feed the newspaper microfiche, how to scroll from day to day, beginning the first of February 1967. A few min-utes later, there it was, the obituary of an eight-year-old girl, a student at a local Catholic school. I read the announce-ment of the memorial service I had attended thirty-eight years before. I read the names of relatives I had sat with. At the end of the article I got what I came for: the name of the cemetery.

It was on the outskirts of town, in a place that was always quiet in the middle of the day. I parked my car on the side of the road, then systematically worked my way across rows of headstones, looking for Bridget's. Three-quarters of the way through, I found it. A pillow marker. A simple block of granite commemorating a brief and consequential life.

For me the distinction between what was and what should have been has blurred beyond recognition, and foiled even my own stubborn faith. All I carry with me is a kaleidoscope of feelings, a conviction to get them down on paper, and the sense of peace that results when I have communicated something true and unobscured by static detail—when I have helped an otherwise forgotten little girl to live forever.

I stood over the monument. A dusty curtain appeared. Beneath it, white shoes and stockings came into view. The curtain eased open.

The eyelashes. The way she clutched the hem of her dress.

You have to go now, Steve. You can't keep waiting for me.

I reached into my pocket. Out came a penny. Its luster had long since faded, but the date was still clear. A faint halo of green oxidation circled its outer edge. I wedged the penny into the soil next to the monument, pressing down with my thumb to sink it as deeply as possible. Then I said goodbye and walked back to my car.

The Evolution of Your Goodbyes

Ruth Schiffmann

he day your father forgets your name doesn't come out of nowhere. You see it coming over weeks, months, and years. There's the day he orders pizza and can't remember the address of the house he's lived in for forty-five years. The morning he pours orange juice in a bowl and drinks with a spoon. The afternoon you arrive at his house to find him wearing two pairs of pants, five shirts, and two hats. With every detail that slips from his grasp you feel the moment that he will forget you approaching like a dreaded, unavoidable fate.

So you try to outrun it. You do this by cooking. You cook in large batches, lining plastic dishes on counter tops and spooning stews and slotted spoonfuls of vegetables into multi-sectioned plates. You label each container in bold blue print, and build leaning towers of stacked covered dishes in your freezer until the next trip to your parents' house, when you will carefully rebuild the towers in their freezer.

After each daily visit, your father walks you from the dining room, carrying the empty plastic dishes down the back steps and to the car. He waits for you to get in, closes the door, and hesitates at the open window. His eyes are wide and bright. You feel him holding you close with his gaze, searching for words that he can't quite find until finally they come. "I'm glad you came," he says, and you know that he's dredged the words from deep in his heart.

Suddenly you are glad that large, dark sunglasses are back in style. You slip them on and start the engine. As he heads back to the house, breaking into a jog to make sure he's at the picture window before you back down the driveway, your heart hurts knowing that you mean that much to him. Before he's out of view, your eyes fill. The tears on your face fall off your chin, and you're relieved that from the window where he's waving to you like a five-year-old, he can only see you smiling from behind movie star sunglasses.

Each day that he greets you by name is a gift to you and a triumph to him. You realize that he's using your name deliberately to test himself, or maybe to keep himself from letting you slip away.

The day comes when you gather the empty plates and head for the door, but he doesn't rise to walk you to your car. You know that there is no other reason than he has forgotten that it is what he usually does. As you climb into your car your chest is a little heavier, your brow knit a little tighter and suddenly, you wish you had hugged him and told him that you loved him. But that's not the kind of family you were. Or are. Instead you back down the driveway, look for him at the window, smile and return his exuberant wave.

The months go by and then suddenly one day you are stunned when he utters a complete sentence. It blindsides you as you realize how long it's been since he's strung words together or joined in a conversation. You wonder where the words have gone, how you could have missed them stealing away. Until you look back, reexamine the visits of a handful of months and recall the struggle in his voice as he fought to keep them from dropping off.

Finally, as you leave one day you can't help yourself. You hug him. He won't even know it's unusual, you think. You will hug him and he will think that's what you do. You wrap your arms around his frail body, feel the sharp angles of his shoulder blades, but he doesn't hug you back. Doesn't know how.

One warm spring day as you sit together in the living room listening to an Elvis CD, you suggest going for a walk. He's on his feet in an instant, following you to the coat closet, eager and excited. As you lead his arm into the sleeve of his sweatshirt he reaches out for you. A hug? you wonder. But then you realize, he is dancing. With you. And it doesn't matter that you are not that kind of family. A family that dances. Because he is smiling and holding your hand and enjoying the music. So you forget about the sweatshirt, and the walk. You take his other hand and dance.

You hold on to the days as long as you can. You serve him lunch on a tray as he sits in his recliner, but have to remind him how to pick up his fork and bring it to his mouth. He

17

falls asleep after a few bites. It takes two of you to get him, half asleep, from the chair to his bed. Elvis is singing in the background, but today you're not dancing.

Eventually, your visits find you signing in at a reception desk, asking strangers to punch numbers into a keypad to unlock doors. Both of you are content to sit and smile at one another while Bing Crosby sings "You Are My Sunshine" and Frank Sinatra croons "Strangers in the Night." It strikes you that he hasn't called you by your name in a very long time, but he still brightens at the sight of your face. As the song ends, your father echoes Frank's "dooby dooby doo," and you both laugh. He holds your gaze and you wish you could read his mind. When you leave you hug him, tell him you will be back soon, and always, always you say, "I love you."

Daddy's Request

Molly Lemmons

I grew up during the 1950s when bleaching your hair was the big thing, especially with teenagers. But my parents grew up in a time when a "lady" did not color her hair.

"The Lord gave you beautiful hair. Don't ever change it," Mother admonished. And Daddy was just as adamant. They viewed a woman with dyed hair in the same way we would later view a girl with pierced ears!

When Mother died in 1997, she and Daddy had been married sixty-four years. Lost and alone, Daddy became blind, and at age ninety, had to sell his house and move to an assisted living apartment. It was then, with great caution, I decided to see if blondes really do have more fun.

Although my conscience was slightly disturbed, I chose to take a chance. After all, I reasoned, my parents would never know. Mother had gone home, and Daddy wouldn't

19

ever see it. I was a grown woman and could make my own choices, couldn't I?

I made the big change. A few weeks after I became a blonde, Daddy fell gravely ill. Even though he was ninety-four and blind, his mind was sharp and witty, his words full of quips and wisdom. But his systems were shutting down from being "plain ole tired," he told me, chuckling.

He told me, "Belle, I nearly died last night, and you know what? It was a wonderful feeling. Nothing hurt and all was peace and beauty. I don't know why anyone would fear death."

They called me at work to come quickly; he was sinking fast. I couldn't believe my ears since I had sat and visited with him only a couple of days earlier. On that day, when I had started to leave, I had hugged him and said, "Bye, Daddy." He'd said, "Oh, is that *you*, Belle?"

"Who did you think it was, Daddy?"

"I didn't know," he answered. "I was just playing along, but now that I know it's you, sit back down and stay a while longer." Sometimes he couldn't recognize my voice as his hearing had gotten worse, too.

Arriving in his room now, I could hear his breathing before I went in. I bent over to kiss him, and he said, "Belle, what have you done to your hair?"

My heart skipped a beat. To respect him all these years— I am well into my sixties—and then to disappoint him in death broke my heart. I suddenly remembered how doctors say that near the end, the hearing is sharpened and the sight becomes keen.

"Daddy, do you mean you can see my hair?"

"I shore can."

"What does it look like to you?"

"It looks like white fuzz, and I'll bet your mother is having a wall-eyed fit. I believe if I were you, I'd put it back."

I kissed Daddy goodbye. Those were the last words he ever spoke.

I put my hair back the next week.

Intersections

Kate Dernocoeur

t was midafternoon on a Wednesday in January when the phone rang. The winter light through the windows was clinical white, and I was alone in the house. It was the doctor.

"Just wanted to let you know," he began. I could sense warmth in his voice, a smile. I sat up straighter, pressed the receiver against my ear. "Your pregnancy test was positive."

It is a cruel and relentless joke, infertility. Anyone I've met—then or since—who is stuck in this unwelcome club calls it infertility shit, and for us, six years after our wedding, four years since we started "trying," it was finally over. Recent weeks of fatigue and a sudden aversion to the smell of diesel and the taste of radishes vindicated years of taking my basal temperature before moving in the morning, charting hormonal currents, love-making on a schedule, one surgery for Jim, two for me.

No more would we have to endure the probing questions: "When you gonna have kids? You guys are trying... aren't you?" Or the outright push—"Have you heard? Mary's daughter is having another baby!"—from parents pressured by the notion of grandparenting.

The day of the phone call, Jim was away on business. He wouldn't be home until Saturday, and I wanted to tell him in person. Although I was at home by myself, I realized I was not alone. It was me and—who? A girl? A boy? Didn't matter. I nicknamed whoever it was "The Cub" and for those several days, it was just the two of us. I laughed, cried, danced to gentle music, imagining the days and years ahead.

❦

A couple of weeks later, my mother's right kidney was removed. A biopsy had suggested cancer. I wonder now why something that in most families would create a tsunami of concern barely caused a ripple in ours. Maybe it was because she was a surgical veteran: two total hip replacements, knee surgery, ankle surgery. In typical fashion, she had shrugged off the news that the blood in her urine would involve an operation that would leave her with a scar that looked like they tried to cut her in half. Her philosophy, and thus ours, was that they'd take out the kidney and that would be that.

The evening before the surgery, we visited her in the hospital. She was pale, and seemed small lying against the white sheets. The head of the bed was raised and she was resting, but as soon as she saw us, she transformed into her favorite role: hostess. First came her famous smile, then the inevitable questions: How are you? What's new? Are you going to the mountains this weekend? I'd long since figured out her method—pitching questions until they led to an interesting conversation. I interrupted her.

"There's something we want you to know before tomorrow," I said. I was probably sitting on the edge of her bed, might even have been holding her hand. By then, I had learned to touch people, to hug, things I'd never done willingly as a kid.

She looked at me, curious, her eyes squinting a little. "Okay..." she said, pulling the word out.

"Well, it's just that normally, we'd wait another month or so before telling," I said, "but in September, you're going to be a grandma."

—————◊/◊/◊—————

My mother's name was Janet. I began calling her that, usually, instead of "Mom" after she remarried and took on four grown stepchildren who called her by name. By the time 1986 rolled around, I was thirty-two, and time had ironed out most of the wrinkles of my childhood. We were both too busy with our adult lives to hold grudges over old bumps and bruises.

The pathology report after surgery suggested that her cancer was gone. We were told there was no need for chemo, no need for radiation. With her typical get-on-with-it approach to life, Janet regained her strength and resumed her routines. As she healed that spring and summer, my own

25

abdomen swelled until we were finally able to share the news with everyone. I quit my job as a paramedic—it was not worth the risk of being out in the knife and gun club of the Denver streets.

"Let's do a mother-daughter overnight before the baby arrives," she said in August, "just the two of us." We had started doing such things now and then. I had even started looking forward to them.

So we booked a night at a bed-and-breakfast in the Colorado foothills. The plan was to leave the city midafternoon, poke around the town of Evergreen, eat out, and spend the night in a cabin by a river outside town. It would be a relief to escape the searing heat of Denver.

It was only a thirty-minute drive, but she must have asked me the same question four times. It might have been about whether I knew the way to the B&B, or what names we were thinking for the baby. I knew the way, and she knew we had decided not to reveal the names we were considering until we told the baby first—she'd known that for weeks. I remember thinking, "Why is she asking me this again?"

Then, when we were browsing the quaint shops in town, a different question got stuck on recycle. I'd answer, we'd wander some more, then she'd repeat the question. At dinner, it happened again. She would ask something, maybe about whether we had purchased a certain stroller, or my next doctor's appointment. I'd answer, we'd eat some, and then again, the same question. It got annoying.

After dinner, I sat on the porch of the cabin as daylight faded, watching the stream. My feet were perched on the porch railing, and I lounged as comfortably as I could beneath my near-term baby belly. There had been some upset words, and I was trying to calm down by slowly breathing the mountain air tinged with the scent of pine.

Janet was fussing inside the cabin; I could hear her moving around, perhaps unpacking. Everything felt off-kilter. Was it then that the word "Alzheimer's" first invaded my mind? Well, her birthday was just a couple of weeks away, and she was turning sixty. Birthdays were always a big deal and this one involved extra-big plans. Her brother was even flying in from Massachusetts. After her birthday, I thought, I'll think about this again.

At bedtime, things were more cordial, but still strained. Just before we turned off the wall lamp hanging precariously on the varnished pine paneling, Janet suddenly turned and walked over to me like a penitent with an offering. She thrust a small white box into my hands and mumbled some words about wanting me to have something special to remember this time of my life, meaning, I think, the part where I was about to become a mother myself.

Inside, I found the beautiful, thick, gold-link bracelet chain with a disk charm that I had always loved on her. I had never imagined I'd own it. My father had given it to her around the time I was born, she said, and now she wanted me to have it. To this day, I regret not thanking her fittingly when I put it around my wrist.

<hr />

Janet was the daughter of a prominent Massachusetts banker, an ancestor of Mayflower stock and Revolutionary War generals. As such, she dutifully learned the rules of society: be a good daughter (more than that—be a perfect daughter); join the Junior League (better yet, be an officer); stage a memorable social debut (and be the most dazzling girl at the debutante party).

She was in the generation of young women in the 1940s who were allowed to go to college, but not encouraged to do too well. She went for an associate's degree from Briarcliff Junior College, where she was a member of the choir and the chorus, and served on both the Athletic Board and the War Service Board. She was president of the freshman class and edited the yearbook senior year. But most importantly, she went there because she could easily get away to the Yale or Princeton football game, or up to Williams for the weekend.

The real job of college girls in those days was to find a man, get married, have babies. She had an impressive string of boyfriends with good names. Janet chose my father after just six dates one romantic Cape Cod summer because he was dashing, and because it was still patriotic for a girl to marry a soldier home from the war. My father married her because she was the most beautiful, the most popular, and always the most fun at a party. At their wedding in 1950, her satin dress was rimmed with pearls, and they were each surrounded by seven attendants. There was a printed guide to the festivities that swirled for days around the main event. The nuptials were mentioned in the *Worcester Telegram*, the *Boston Globe*, the *New York Times*.

But then came the dusty brown of west Texas, where her husband's work took them. The demands of his newly founded company meant he was seldom home, and when the kids came—my brother in Dallas, and me, two years later in Denver—the belle of the ball was two thousand miles from anything familiar. She was terrified of the fragility of babies, of my toddler brother, of the specter of germs in the era of polio.

———◊/◊/◊———

When my own husband proposed marriage, we were camping for five days in Colorado's San Juan Mountains. We were standing on the Continental Divide on a windless summer evening. Maybe it's best that the camera malfunctioned and only in my mind's eye can I still see the hues of an unusually grand sunset.

I don't remember Jim's exact words, but when "married" was one of them I was only mildly surprised. I'd met Jim seven months earlier, when I was new to the Denver Paramedic Division and he had moved into a room in the household I was sharing with a couple of other medics. As we went from being roommates to being in love, he was resoundingly clear about one thing: "I want kids. The woman I marry has to want kids, too."

Jim grew up in a place alien to me: a happy, loving home. None of his family lore involved shouting or fighting, was ever about tension or meanness. In his stories, dinner never ended in abrupt, angry departures from the table. The children were not sent off as a matter of routine to boarding school.

"Who would send a child away?" he said. "Why would anyone want to do that?"

"It was just how things were. It was normal," I tried to explain. I grew up expecting to go to boarding school. I looked forward to it. Boarding school was my ticket out.

"Why wouldn't you want to see your own kids grow up?" he asked.

Why indeed.

So by the time his proposal at sunset on the Continental Divide came along, I—who had never wasted time as a little girl imagining my wedding day or entertaining the notion of being a wife or mother—had learned that happy, close, loving families weren't just *Leave It To Beaver* lies. His parents had chosen to have seven children for no better reason than because they loved them. Children there weren't simply part of the script, a byproduct, a nuisance. They didn't know that they should be seen and not heard.

At sunset on the Continental Divide, I was ready. I said, "Yes."

<hr />

When I was six, my family moved to New England from Colorado. We lived in a cozy red farmhouse on Ingham Hill Road. There were neighbors, lots of kids, softball games in the goat pasture. There were paths in the woods, and Concord grapes you could reach from your bike along the road in fall, and a horse up the street that you could ride if you could catch it. There were sledding parties, birthday parties, skating parties on the pond.

When I was a kid, my mother worked a self-appointed job: full-time volunteer. In those times, it was the only option for a woman like her. Nature centers, Girl Scouts, Planned Parenthood, other causes consumed her time and attention. Before email or answering machines, she had a knack for pulling off fundraisers and consciousness-raising campaigns. Because of this, she was perpetually on the phone, twirling a clump of hair around her middle finger, around and around. She did it without realizing. The more intense the telephone conversation, the faster the finger twirled around the snatch of bobbed hair.

When I was in elementary school, I imagined that I could be the one to help her break this annoying habit. "Don't twirl your hair!" I'd stage-whisper as I brushed past her on my way in from the school bus, my book bag bumping her sort of on purpose. She never greeted the school bus. I think she meant to. Instead, she tried to fit in just one more phone call. I'd walk in and there she'd be, standing beside her cluttered desk next to our cramped dining room, phone to her ear, twirling her hair. She might raise her eyebrows in silent greeting and throw me a smile, or maybe not. She seldom sat down, just hovered over the mess of papers, leaned over now and then to make notes. Did other mothers bake cookies and have a snack with their kids when they came in from school? That wasn't her thing.

When I was twelve, my grandfather died and suddenly we could afford a big gray stone house on tony River Road that my father had admired for years. It wasn't visible from the road—the sweeping, curving driveway was a third of a

mile long—but he'd seen it from his boat when he was doing research on the Connecticut River. To my parents, it was
a dwelling worthy of their birthright, but gone for me were
the sledding hill, the nearby friends, the skating pond, the
neighborhood horse.

It was the era of nightly cocktails. I grew up hearing
the chink-tinkle of ice filling a highball glass and the drone
of conversation punctuated by high-pitched laughter. My
mother had a way of turning every gathering into a good
party. The role of hostess filled her up. When she entered a
room, heads always turned to see who had come in. From
the edge of things, I always wondered how she did it.

At River Road, cocktails were served on a silver tray, either out on one of the gray stone patios in good weather or
in the large living room with floor-to-ceiling windows if the
weather was bad. Either way, the river view was perfect.

Because my brother was already away at boarding school,
I was the only kid around. I'd take a break from homework,
wander into the party, say hello. I did this half out of bore-
dom and half because it was expected of me. I could have
perfect manners and still be thinking how much I hated being asked what I wanted to be when I grew up. After a while,
I turned it into a private game: I'd drum up future identities
that I never intended—lawyer, doctor, aeronautical engineer.
I could say anything, and did, and still the guests would nod,
smile, act impressed. And ask me again at the next party.

Somehow I knew even as a kid that this was all a script
for my parents' generation. Grow up, go to college, get married, have kids, live happily ever after. During the fifties and

early sixties, everyone was trying to measure up to an impossible ideal. I was just part of an agenda, a vague social obligation.

Much later, when I was married and Janet somehow imagined I'd understand, we had a talk. I don't remember how she broached the subject, but I know there was no careful build-up. She just launched into it, like a confession: she hadn't wanted a second child. She hadn't wanted the baby who became me.

I wasn't surprised. Somehow, I had always known that had Janet married twenty years later, after the hippies and the women's movement and *Roe v. Wade*, I would never have happened at all. Intellectually, from the perspective of a grown woman, I could sympathize with what being a young mother had been like for her, coping with her disillusionment and my difficult brother, and west Texas. I could understand not wanting another child when the one you have is running roughshod over you in a place without friends or family. She told me how she had done things like push a heavy car out of the mud, exercise viciously, hit herself. I came anyway.

My mother never got over not wanting that pregnancy, tried hard to make up for it. She'd drive three hours to visit me at summer camp, watch me ride in horse shows. My friends all loved how attentive she was to them, how she always arrived with coolers brimming with picnic fixings. "Your mom is so cool!" they'd say. I'd wish I could agree, but even then there was a dead place inside where feeling treasured should have been.

———— ❦ ————

Three weeks after the overnight in Evergreen, the big six-tieth birthday weekend was finally upon us. I hadn't spoken to Janet much since then, mostly because I knew I'd see her that Friday—September 12—for lunch. A long-time friend had proposed a quiet get-together at her home in the country, just the three of us, before the weekend's bigger festivities.

I arrived at noon. Cynthia and I chatted a few minutes, then went to her patio to wait for Janet. A half hour later, no Janet. We went to the kitchen telephone to call her house. No answer. We returned to the patio.

In another half hour, we'd run out of baby things to chat about, and I must have said, "Well, this isn't like Mom to be so late. I know she was planning to be here. We talked about it yesterday."

Could there have been an accident? A flat tire?

We called my stepfather. He hadn't heard from her.

"You know," said Cynthia, "I hope she's OK. She's been sort of...odd lately."

I nodded. I had noticed. We began to compare notes. Janet had been forgetful. There were inappropriate outbursts. I told Cynthia how she kept repeating herself in Evergreen. The idea of calling the Alzheimer's people after the birthday weekend returned to mind. I rested my forty-weeks-distended belly on my lap, felt hot and more than a little bothered.

Finally, she wandered in. We heard her enter the house, and we turned to greet her. And then she said in a small voice, "Am I late?"

As she came out into the light of the patio, I remember thinking, she looks so frail, so confused. Clearly, she was exhausted.

"Where have you been?" I was relieved, angry, baffled.

"I don't know. I just couldn't seem to get here." She'd been coming to this house for decades.

She sat. We sat. No one knew what to say, there on the patio, framed by the cloudless Colorado sky. To say "something seems wrong" would alter our world. The day was too nice. This was supposed to be a celebration.

After a lifetime in which Janet was the go-to woman, I tried convincing myself that this wasn't happening. I remember thinking, Why doesn't she take charge? I had a sensation of being on a threshold I didn't want to cross. I sat frozen. Our hostess clearly didn't feel it was her business to take the lead, so it fell to me. How to begin? All I could do was push over the edge—falling off a waterfall must be easier. Finally, I said, "Mom, something's not right."

We talked. I could tell she had probably known something was wrong in the three weeks since our overnight, but hadn't dared admit it, even to herself.

"I'll call Dr. Eiseman," I finally said, getting up. Contacting our close family friend, a surgeon, was always a first step at a time like this. I left Janet, looking alarmingly tiny in her deck chair, in the sun with Cynthia, and retreated to the kitchen.

I got through to Dr. Eiseman right away. Standing there, linked by the phone cord to a person I knew I could trust, I explained what had happened. I told him about Janet's changing personality over the past few weeks, about her being late and confused, about how exhausted she seemed. His reply was unhesitant: "This is metastatic brain cancer until proven otherwise."

The cool, dim kitchen exploded bright and hot. He's got to be overreacting, I thought. How can he say such a thing?

But he was so sure. Somehow, I got back out to the deck. "Mom, he said to come to the hospital."

———

The silence during the drive was broken only by the fan set high, blowing cold. The windows were up, and in the passenger seat a woman I barely recognized sat still, like an obedient child, staring ahead, hands folded in her lap. We did not speak. When I glanced sideways at her, I could see nothing of the woman who was my mother, only an abruptly ancient person. She was as unfamiliar as a hitchhiker. Ahead, the asphalt shimmered in the mid-September Colorado sun, but we were chilled by the air conditioning and the unknown.

A few hours later, I leaned against the wall of a side hallway where I'd ducked away from the rest of the ER for a few minutes. The cool ceramic tiles felt good, siphoning the heat off my back. I had told my mother I was going to see whether the CT scan was back, but really, I just needed a break. Because the head of the emergency department was my husband's boss, because the director of nursing was a close friend, because I had come through those doors a thousand times in my own work as a paramedic, it had been an overwhelming parade of well-wishers wearing their professional game faces.

But it was quiet that Friday, and the ER was dead. The CT scan of my mother's head seemed to be the most interesting thing going on. It would arrive soon, and nurses, doctors, even clerks, were gathering nearby.

I wrapped my arms around my belly, held it like a schoolgirl's armload of books. I was full-term, due Monday. I flattened my aching low back against the cool tiles. For a few minutes, I stood motionless, staring vaguely at something far away in the off-white linoleum floor.

Someone in a white lab coat arrived with the films and slipped them into the opaque clips of the backlight with that unmistakably efficient sound. The group pressed forward to see the film. They were huddled in front of me, and I had to stand on tiptoe to see.

"Look at that..." someone muttered. Even to the untrained eye, the two large tumors were obvious, like translucent white eggs nestling in the murky shadows of her brain.

Time, motion, sound stopped. For a moment, there was only that hallway, and the ghostly light, and the people staring into it, mesmerized. Then the group disbanded, walking past me, eyes down, summoned by sudden and indistinct urgencies.

——⟨•/•/•⟩——

As I leaned against the cool tiles of the ghostly hallway, what I had been trying to see was the future. I wondered what it would be like to see my child learn to smile, to sit, get teeth, speak, feed herself, walk. At the same time, I wondered what it would be like as Janet gradually stopped speaking, walking, feeding herself. She would eventually just sit, then stay in bed all the time, become increasingly vacant. One day, she would be gone.

The birthday parties were cancelled, of course. The oncologist started radiation and they gave her diuretics and other medications, returning Janet to near-normal by the end of the week. My due date came and went, but it didn't matter. On Wednesday, I arrived to take Janet for radiation, only to discover she had walked away from the hospital. The police found her four hours later, sleeping on the porch of a house four blocks away.

By Friday, Janet was like new. "You ready to go home?" I asked, and was rewarded by a clear-eyed, rested, with-it, "Yes!" She was walking strongly and the vagueness was gone. There was a lightness to the day that went beyond the perfect weather. We settled her at home in the care of my stepdad. Then Jim and I went home for some time to ourselves. That evening, we were watching a movie when my turn came. We drove back to Rose Hospital, so I could be admitted to Labor and Delivery. The next day, at 8:08 p.m., I became a mother.

⚜

Was there something to it that Janet, who always loved a good party, died on St. Patrick's Day? Was there something to it that we buried her ashes three days later, on the first day of spring, the day my daughter was eighteen months old? Every year, these dates loom large. Every year, I think about that pivotal time.

The morning Janet died, I planned to be with her at the inpatient hospice where she'd been for six months, but the babysitter was late. The morning was warm, spring-like. Sunlight was streaming in the kitchen's bay window when I answered the phone at about 9:30. When I hung up after hearing the news, the sun had disappeared, obscured by a sudden shower of huge white snowflakes, like a snow globe. Each flake wavered back and forth, slowly, dropped lightly to the ground. For just a couple of minutes, the snow shower filled the bay window, and then it was gone, like a whisper.

The Sea Monster

Iwona Tokc-Wilde

othing, absolutely nothing, could have spoilt that summer's day. My six-year-old self was oblivious to the throngs of half-naked bodies, rhythmically spit-turning in the roasting sun; the odd cigarette end between my sand-encrusted toes; the bad man up on the dunes, relieving himself in the long grass.

I was oblivious to my little brother's pleading to help him with his sand castle. I was oblivious to everything but the sea: soup-warm with peaks of salty cream, murky-gray, forever shifting and a little dangerous. Like a flying fish, I was in and out, rejoicing under Mother's watchful eye, conscious that soon it would be time to go home again.

But she hadn't paid attention, not really, not when the sea monster invited my little brother in. The sea monster held onto Peter tight, baptizing him one more time, playing a game of tug-of-war with Mother until she promised it the world. They made a pact that day, the sea monster and Mother, and someone was going to have to pay.

Peter grew up loving the sea, the memory of that day eluding him. He made a few promising sketches at the art college and checked into his first rehab at the age of eighteen. By the time he was twenty-five he nearly drowned in the bathtub twice, fell through frozen ice once, and walked into the sea several times. Heroin did this. Or was it the sea monster? I moved away, putting another sea between me and my family, and didn't want to know.

Cocooned in my own house by my own sea, I watched the years go by, hideous in their ordinariness. Peter was often on my mind, but I didn't want to know.

Mother met a clinician once, who told her some people are born this way: "A gene or two gone wrong creates a human being predisposed to addiction and habitual behavior." They push the self-destruction button over and over again. Mother didn't tell him about the sea monster. I didn't tell her Peter's life was not worth living.

There was hope once, when Peter told Mother he got a girl pregnant. I had not seen him for a few years but started planning a trip back home, hoping for a new beginning, hoping to get to know my brother at last. But there was no pregnancy and no girlfriend, only an unpaid debt and a gun to Peter's head. What else? I didn't want to know.

I did go back, once, for Mother's sixtieth birthday. And he was there, my little brother, only not so little any more, and not my brother any more. He was temporarily sober, out of another rehab, but I didn't know him at all.

I got a glimpse of what he might have been when we went to the beach once more, the two of us, alone. Nothing, absolutely nothing, could have spoilt that summer's day. I watched as he sketched, the greenish expanse before us pulsating. Out of sight, the sea monster was watching, too.

It was the last time I saw this man I never knew. Peter took his own life a year later. I crossed the sea again.

I watched Mother wash his body, his arms and legs stick-thin, ravaged by years of neglect. I watched her tears caress his emaciated face, so lovingly and tenderly. She unclasped the sea monster's clutches and her little boy was hers again. She baptized him once more, in death.

How I wished I had known my brother, the broken man he was. I wished I'd told him I loved him despite it all. I wished I'd told him his life was worth living because my mother loved him even more.

We took his ashes to the sea and nothing spoilt that summer's day. The ocean of blue and calm, inviting and comforting, was not the least dangerous, the sea monster gone.

The pact had run its course, the price was paid, the long day had ended. I could see them on the beach: Peter, whose life was never truly lived; my mother, whose grief began that day thirty years before; and my six-year-old self, who didn't know.

Now my mother is broken, staring into the sea alone, and I know she would have those thirty years back, and more. I think I'll stay. I will not go back to my house on the distant shore.

Benediction:
Mom's Last Scrabble Game

Betty Jo Goddard

hen someone dies, I suppose it's human nature to wish we'd done things differently. I wish I had stayed in Illinois when I was there in June of 1995, but I was in a stew to get back to Alaska to start my garden. When I left Illinois, I didn't know Mom would be dead three weeks later.

Right before I left to drive back to Alaska, I massaged Mom's sagging arms and bony, bent back. When I turned to leave, Mom opened her arms to me, and I hugged her good-bye. Always before when I left, she said, "Well, when are you coming to see me again?"

This time she didn't. Instead, as I hugged her, she said, "Goodbye, my first-born. I loved you then, I love you now, and I'll love you to the end."

Did she know?

45

I'd barely had time to plant my garden when the message came. "Mom's dying," my brother Jim said.

"I'll pack my car tonight and start for Illinois tomorrow. How much time do you think she has?"

"Better fly out if you want to see her alive. She won't last long."

With my mind, I rushed the plane toward Illinois. As we thrummed over checkerboard farmland, regret chided me. I wished I had given Mom more time, talked to her as an equal, treated her as a person of substance capable of understanding and responding thoughtfully and intelligently.

Oh, we kids acknowledged Mom—the work she'd done, her independence, her enterprise, her appreciation of nature. Yet we, her children, treated her as a child. With a chuckle of superiority, we joked about things she did and said. We listened to her with contained, often amused, impatience when she told us what to do. Then we told her what she should do, what was good for her, how she should live her life.

To her credit, as long as she was able, Mom usually went ahead and did things the way she wanted to.

But when, I wondered as I flew over cloud blankets toward St. Louis, did I show Mom true respect and honoring?

Three weeks earlier, I had honored Mom's intelligence by playing Scrabble with her. That was non-threatening, and we both enjoyed it. When we played Scrabble, I had no difficult rejoinders to phrase, no uncomfortable questions to respond to. All playing Scrabble with Mom required was patience and humor.

Before I drove off for Alaska, Mom and I played one last

Scrabble game. Mom was almost too weak to play, but still, she wanted to. She struggled out of her chair and, gasping and panting, pegged her walker the two or three steps to the kitchen, where I was clattering around. "How about a game?" she said.

Is she trying to give me a good time? I wondered. Is she bidding for togetherness? Or does she really want to play?

I looked at my stooped, wasted, ninety-two-year-old mother standing panting in the kitchen doorway, gripping her walker and looking up at me through her thick cataract glasses. "Are you sure you want to, Mom?" I asked.

"Oh, yes, I want to," Mom said with certainty. So I got out the Scrabble board and we played.

Mom took ages to play. I straightened the house, cooked, did dishes, and worked a crossword puzzle while she studied and restudied her tiles. Time and again, she dropped tiles on the floor and had me recover them. As I groped around underneath her chair, she lifted one blue-tinged foot at a time and wiggled it a bit, in case an elusive tile was hidden in the furry confines of her pink bedroom slippers.

Sometimes she dozed during her turn. When I spoke to her, she awakened with a start and said, "Oh, is it my turn?" Then, breathing shallowly through her sagging, open mouth, she recommenced fingering her tiles and studying them, fingering and studying.

Usually, when we played Scrabble, I won. But this game—Mom's last Scrabble game—Mom drew good tiles. She got the X, the J, the Z, the Q, the K, all four S's, and both blanks. She worked her small victories: triple word scores. She pulled her usual trick with the X, pushing it onto a two-way triple letter score.

Then, after a long period of snoozing, studying, and moving her tiles around, Mom laid down all seven of her tiles in one play. That boosted her—a fifty-point bonus! She didn't ask what the score was, but she was leaving me in the dust.

I placed my futile effort on the board, then busied myself with the vacuum while waiting for Mom's next play.

Time passed. Earth rotated. Sun moved westward. I peeled supper potatoes and waited.

"Okay, I'm ready," Mom's rattly voice called.

I put down my paring knife and went to see what Mom would play.

I could hardly believe it. On the heels of her last fifty-point bonus, Mom did it again! With a shaky hand, she spilled all seven of her tiles onto the board and maneuvered them into place. There it was: A second unchallengeable seven-letter word attached with an S to a five-letter word.

I shrieked, *"Twice in a row! Mom!"*

I watched Mom. She was too weak to exclaim over her feat. But I saw her pink bedroom slippers wave a bit and a little wiggle of pleasure go through her. Mom received her benediction in that—her last game of Scrabble. I was glad.

Love Letters

Mary E. McIntyre

A heavy box bound with shiny packing tape is cornered on the top shelf of Dad's bedroom cupboard. I tilt the box, flipping my head away from an explosion of gray dust, and heft the contents in my hands down to the floor.

"This is the last thing, Dad."

Dad and I are nearing the end of an invasive sorting process. It's an essential step for deciding what he will need in a retirement home after his cherished home of forty-two years goes up for sale in a few weeks. He slumps on one side of the mattress beside the walnut headboard, the familiar place he shared with Mum for sixty-one years.

Macular degeneration keeps him from seeing the box, but he knows what weighs so heavily on the floor between us. Speechless with grief, he sinks his head further into his chest and raises a shaky hand to his eyes. I sit beside him and put my arm around his shoulders. He pulls out a hanky, wipes his nose and struggles for composure.

"I promised your mother I'd burn them."

I try to hide my alarm. The letters my parents wrote to each other during World War II bulge inside the box. To them the contents are personal notes from Dad's wartime posting to the Halifax shipyards, but to me they are keys for unlocking family secrets. Their stories in their own hand-writing are taped away from prying eyes, stories about my older siblings' births and babyhood, Mum's life under her parents' roof, Dad's work as a Chief Petty Officer for the Royal Canadian Navy. It is as if all of the codes, the answers, the history, and the understanding of a senseless war will be revealed to me by simply opening the box.

I've known of their promise to each other for years, but still hope I can change Dad's mind. Surely Dad, who sits with me daily in the sunroom drinking cups of tea and re-vealing layers of his childhood, his work, and his family, can't burn the proof of his history. And Mum—lost to us forever just one month ago—would her memory still hold him to his pact to sever the connecting threads?

"Dad, can we leave this for now? Let's talk about what to do with it later."

I'm buying time. I want to soften his resolve and some-how convince him of the letters' importance to the rest of the family. What I most want is to capture the emotion of those days before I was born in 1947. I have plenty of memories of grandparents and aunts and uncles in the 1950s, but I want to know what came before.

I understand Mum's reasons for the deathbed pact with Dad. At times of great fear and yearning, she'd written love letters she did not want a lover to reveal to anyone else. Imagine the embarrassment of pet names and syrupy protestations of love exposed to an unsympathetic span of time. Or worse, imagine no opportunity to explain what possessed her to risk writing her feelings on paper. But this understanding doesn't keep me from hoping Dad will relent. For years I have been obsessed with capturing family history through old photographs and letters, and now I secretly challenge my mother's final request to burn their secrets.

For two weeks, the sealed box teases me from the bedroom floor. I suggest to Dad that I read the letters to him one last time before he takes steps to burn them. He says it will make him too sad. I offer to stow them in the locker at the retirement home in case he might want to read them another day. No, that would be dragging too much of the sad past forward. And he reminds me he has made a promise.

Living with Dad and managing his affairs after Mum's death has taken me away from my own life. I arrange for my brother to stay with Dad one day while I catch up with my other responsibilities. Returning to Dad's house at dinnertime, I notice the normally quiet house feels even more silent. I hang up my coat and turn into the living room. Dad is seated straight and patient in his chair, as if he has taken time to compose himself.

"I have something to tell you," he says.

Puffy red folds rim his tired eyes. I sit opposite his chair, expectant. A problem for me to solve, I guess.

"I know how important the letters are to you," he says.

Dread stiffens my face, an expression he can't see.

"Bob helped me burn them today...in a barrel...in the backyard."

There it is. The message I don't want to hear. At first a sense of loss weighs down on my chest, then rage infuses my mind, like grieving all over again.

My silence is worrying him because his voice quavers when he says, "I'm sorry, but a promise is a promise."

I can't trust my voice not to reveal the disappointment I feel. Angry words of finality spin in my head—irretrievable, irrevocable. But not the word "lost," because that implies the letters can be found.

With shaking hands, he lifts a creased envelope across the space that separates us. An old stamp is cancelled in the corner. I take it.

"Bob held back the last one and asked me if I wanted him to read it to me. He did and I saved it for you."

I lift the yellowing flap, pull out a folded square and read the letter. He called her "Bubs." He hoped his leave would make it possible for him to be home for the christening of their second daughter. He poked fun at his roommate who tried to compliment the landlady into giving him second helpings of pie. He talked of missing her and his first daughter since they'd returned to Toronto to live with her parents during her second pregnancy. He told her the classes of ships he worked on, and reminded her of places they'd visited together when she and my oldest sister lived with him in Halifax for a year. He hoped she would go with her parents to their cottage and get some rest. There is more: shortages, expenses, train schedules, things I can barely read through the tears I push off my cheeks with the back of my hand.

Dad gets up and crosses the room to sit with me on the couch. We hold hands and cry through the sadness. My sympathy for him over the permanent loss of his wife and the letters that meant so much to them is unbearable.

Dad made the right and only choice for him and Mum. I finally understand and respect their shared reluctance to reveal what must have been a special and private time in their lives. A promise is a promise.

The Skid Row Float

Annmarie B. Tait

When I was a kid, accepting castoffs from well-intentioned friends and relatives was a recurring event for my family of seven. Used sofas came and went with regular frequency. The acquisition of a new (old) couch usually coincided with saying the final goodbye to one of my lovely old great-aunts. In fact, the really old aunts avoided us completely if word got around that our sofa was on its last legs. As a child I believed wholeheartedly in Santa Claus, the Easter Bunny, and that receiving the sofa of a deceased relative was part of the funeral rite.

I remember vividly when in the summer of 1964, the good Lord called Aunt Alice home at the ripe age of eighty-seven. Somehow our dear old camel-back, larger-than-life sofa knew it. Secure in the knowledge that a replacement sofa waited in the wings, the "Cranberry Queen of Velveteen," as we fondly referred to it, slipped from the two

55

brick makeshift legs that supported her rear, breathed her last soft sigh, and thumped to the floor right on schedule.

A few days later, as we all gathered to pay our last respects to Aunt Alice, a cloud of silence hung heavily over the congregation—until my annoyingly squeaky yet perfectly audible voice punched a big fat hole in it.

"Mom," I said, "is Daddy going right to Aunt Alice's house now to pick up the couch or do we have to wait until the cemetery part is over?"

In one fell swoop my mother stretched clear across my four older siblings, clamped my lips shut with one hand, air-lifted me back past the four siblings with the other, and plunked me down at her side. Time elapsed: three-tenths of a nanosecond. While in flight I caught my dad clamping his own mouth shut and I wondered what that was about. After all he hadn't uttered a word. I knew something was up, though, because a series of muffled giggles rippled through the crowd.

Personally, I saw no humor in the situation at all, let alone any reason for my mother to physically button my lips and pluck me from my seat. Obviously not having anywhere to sit when it was time to watch *The Flintstones* panicked no one but me.

After the funeral service was over (including the cemetery part) Dad headed out to collect Aunt Alice's sofa. Mom's task was to dispose of the wreck in our living room. Because of its deplorable condition, her goal was to haul it to the Goodwill donation station at the end of our block sans fanfare. Frankly, all the good will on Earth couldn't have resurrected this hunk of junk, but the anonymous donor option trumped leaving it for the trash pick up. If she was going to do that she might as well hang a neon sign on it with a blinking arrow pointing to our front door.

The problem: four daughters and one son all under the age of sixteen make a mighty sorry-looking moving crew—especially when pursuing an incognito operation.

With limited options and dripping with anxiety, Mom summoned the courage to recruit my brother Bobby and three of his teenage friends. This decision was so immediately followed by regret, a NASCAR stopwatch couldn't have clocked the time in between.

To Bobby and his band of merry men, carrying an oversized, threadbare, broken down, ugly sofa the length of one city block spelled P-A-R-T-Y. Wise to the antics of teenage boys, Mom suggested they wait until dark. They laughed. She insisted. They picked Mom up and moved her out of the way.

I can still picture those boys lumbering down the alley in single file with that clumsy old couch carcass raised high over their heads, chanting some quirky made-up rhyme. When they finally reached the end of the block Bobby looked back at Mom and shouted, "Hey, look, Mom. It's a parade and we own the Skid Row Float!" Even the long arm of Marie Tait, mother extraordinaire, couldn't reach clear down to the end of the block to lock his lips shut.

The echo of his remark floated down the alley, rustling the curtains of every open kitchen window. By the time his words reached Mom's ears, she couldn't resist laughing out loud as all hope of our anonymity disappeared.

An antique mahogany-trimmed Georgian style sofa stands in all its regal splendor in my living room today. Mom passed it down to me, but it belonged first to my grandmother, who was the last surviving sister in the circle of delightful ladies known to me as my great-aunts. This sofa is not a modern assembly line version. It is a grand tribute to an age when crafting a sofa took several months of a man's life.

"They just don't make them like that anymore." That's what Mom said when she inherited it, threadbare and faded. She decided to have it reupholstered, though by then she could have easily afforded a new sofa.

It's a beauty, all right, and I am comforted by the vintage grace it lends to my living room. But truthfully I own something even better. Mine is the treasure of the "Skid Row Float" and the wealth of heartwarming family memories it rekindles in me. Often material possessions were in short supply at our house. As for memories, we made those by the dozen.

Dawn

Diana M. Amadeo

awn and I originally met as nurse and patient years ago. Then we started seeing each other at our kids' sporting events. As multiple sclerosis took its toll on my body, I had to put my RN career on hold. With the nurse/patient relationship no longer an awkward barrier, we started hanging out.

We were undoubtedly the oddest-looking pair in town. For two years, three days a week, we'd get our children off to school, then meet and have breakfast at a local coffee shop. There, we would solve world problems, discuss local politics, giggle and gossip.

Our presence was always met with stares, often with shock, and occasionally pity. Just thirty years old, Dawn was losing her long battle with breast cancer. She was bloated by steroids, pale and pasty from radiation, and bald from chemo. I was also young, pale, gaunt, and weak, riding an electric wheelchair or dragging my body around with Lofstrand crutches. Yet, we found each other hilarious. Our time together was a welcome break from all the emotional, mental, and physical stress that illness can bring.

New Hampshire's cold wintry holidays had just passed and we were in the midst of a winter thaw. My buddy and I were leaving the restaurant after a heady discussion of the trip we were about to take. Suddenly, Dawn ducked behind me.

"Quick, hide me. There's my mother."

I giggled and shielded her from view. It wasn't that Dawn disliked her mother. She just didn't want to divulge where we were headed lest the woman dissolve into tears. Moms are like that when their daughters are dying.

For the past few months I had been driving us around town. Dawn had reluctantly agreed that her driving days were past. The cancer that began in her breast six years ago had now accelerated rapidly to include bone, lung, and brain. Some days she didn't even know me. I had noticed the shortened attention span, brief episodes of cognitive impairment, and confusion even before she had been informed of brain metastasis. With that new diagnosis came a grave prognosis.

"Thank you for helping me with this," Dawn said as I pulled the van into the church parking lot.

"That's what friends are for," I said hoarsely.

We met the assistant pastor just as he was about to enter his own vehicle.

"We were just coming to talk with you," I said, leaving Dawn to struggle from the van alone.

"Can it wait, Diana?" he asked. "I'm kind of in a hurry." He paused as he saw my friend stagger forward. He knew us well, but he was clearly surprised at Dawn's rapid physical decline. "What do you need help with, Dawn?"

"My funeral," she said, bluntly. There was an awkward silence.

He shut the car door and led us into the rectory. We sat across from him. Slowly, painstakingly, details were worked out. Dawn seemed even more confused and detached than an hour before. I reminded her of the Bible readings she selected and songs that she wanted sung at the service. The reverend's eyes were glistening when he said, "I have seen many things, have heard many stories in this office, but never have I seen the bravery and support of two greater friends. You both are vessels filled with the Holy Spirit."

The following day after the children left for school, I met with Dawn, her husband Doug, and the home hospice nurse. When the time came, Dawn would live out her final days at home surrounded by friends and family. After the nurse and Doug left, I tried to tidy up the kitchen table, but my body was weak and the dishes slipped from my grasp.

As I bent to pick up the broken shards of glass there came an even greater crash. Dawn had fallen.

We worked together, me leaning back on my crutches for leverage, Dawn grasping the heavy couch. It took a good fifteen minutes to raise Dawn from the floor and ease her onto the couch. I called her husband and said she could no longer be alone.

With my nursing background, pastoral care visits to

the homebound, hospital visitations, and grief counseling experience, I thought that parting with my friend would be smooth and graceful. It wasn't. I was subject to sudden bursts of anger toward God, feelings of inadequacy for not being able to help with her physical care, deep depression, and an impending sense of doom. Our relationship was built upon facing illness head-on with mocking irreverence and strength in victory over evil. But now, we were battle weary. I was losing a beautiful, wonderful friend in the worst way possible. For the first time, I was being phony to Dawn— smiling and cheerful to her face and sobbing uncontrollably on the way home.

It sounded rehearsed and hollow when I told her that in spirit she would always be around to watch her kids grow up, since love is eternal. When she whispered, "I love you so very much," my tears started. She was visibly pained by my strug- gle. She'd try to reassure me with, "I will miss you." During an intense exchange, I asked Dawn if just once in a while she would look down on me from Heaven and help me on my life journey. My now blind friend turned her head toward my voice, and with perfectly focused eyes looked straight at me and replied, "No!"

We both started laughing. Soon, we both began to sob. After a while I tried again. "Please?" "No," she teased. And so we went off again. Laughter was our signature through sick- ness, funeral arrangements, and end-stage blindness.

A few days prior to her death, Dawn whispered that she had just seen Jocelyn (a friend from her cancer support group who had died months before). Then she said that Jesus was in the room. I told her that both Jocelyn and Jesus would help her pass when she was ready. I asked her if she understood me. She said, "Yes."

This was the last conversation that we had. To the world she became comatose.

Home alone with my thoughts, I sobbed, wailed, and shouted. I thought of distancing myself to save my own health, but could not. The winter thaw was over and cold air returned. In bed, I tossed and turned, unable to turn off my thoughts. Finally, sleep came. And with sleep came a dream so vivid that it seemed real:

I was at home serving tea to four women about my age and their many children. It was time for the school bus to arrive, and three of the women left to help their kids into their winter coats. However, one woman stayed. While we picked up dishes, she gave me a litany of her problems. She went on and on ad nauseum, until I felt ready to burst. I wanted to shout that she didn't know what real problems were. What she was describing were simply inconveniences. But she rattled on and on and on. The other women and all the children were gone. I was left alone with this annoying woman.

Then I heard a familiar laugh. I looked up, and on my couch sat Dawn. She was young, slim, healthy, and radiant. Her hair was thick and full, with golden ringlets tight around her face. She was wearing a sparkling white gown that flowed over her perfect trim body. She had an amazing big smile and confident twinkling eyes.

"Friends," she said with a chuckle. "You sure know how to pick 'em."

I awoke to an early morning phone call. Doug asked me to come to their home as soon as possible. He sounded lost and sad. I heard sobbing in the background. "Is she gone?" I asked softly. "Yes," he mumbled. "Just a few moments ago."

As I trudged toward Dawn's house one last time, snow began to fall. Noises were muffled, the surrounding air silent. I thought of the Nativity and Christ's birth, celebrated less than a month before. As I held Dawn's still warm hand, I sensed love and new beginnings. For the first time in a long time, I felt peace.

Holding Him Softly

Denise Emanuel Clemen

or the umpteenth time I go over the list. My sister has a five-month-old baby of her own. The aunt who is unable to have children is married to a man who has always said he would never adopt. My cousins are all younger and unmarried.

There is no one who can take the baby.

I ask for a special meeting with the adoption agency. I'm still in hiding—living with a foster family on their farm sixty miles from my home town. After supper, with a thunderstorm brewing, my social worker drives down the gravel road to talk with me. My boyfriend comes too. The three of us sit at the kitchen table while I tell them my latest plan.

"I want the baby to go to a temporary foster family instead of doing a permanent adoption," I say. "I'm staying with a foster family, and I'll go home in a week or so. The baby can do the same thing. It'll just take longer."

My social worker is sitting across from me, and he rests his long arms on the table, looking right at me as I talk.

"We'll start college at the end of August, just like we planned," I say, glancing at my boyfriend. "We'll get engaged at Christmas. Married next summer. Then we'll say we can't have kids, and we want to adopt." They see where I'm heading now.

My boyfriend gets up and paces across the worn linoleum as thunder rumbles low and mean, rattling the kitchen window. He has that look on his face that he's had a lot lately. Like his tie or his shirt collar is strangling him. Only he's wearing a t-shirt. He doesn't say a word. The whole world seems silent and heavy until my foster mother Sarah's voice drifts down the open stairway. "Oh Danny Boy," she croons to her baby Danny, trying to lullaby him to sleep. The social worker reaches out and touches my hand.

"That would be a terrible choice," he says. He sounds sad. Facts and figures stream from his mouth like cold gray rain. I hear words like "attachment" and "bonding" and "trauma." I pray for a lightning bolt to strike all of us dead.

But the next morning, I concede that the social worker is right. And so a day or two later my mother comes to Sarah's house. We are going to see the baby. Unwed mothers in 1970 are not allowed to see their babies—it's supposed to make things easier, people say. But I'm not buying it. My social worker has promised to have the baby at the agency so my mom and I can take a look at him. He's probably only agreed because he thinks I'm on the verge of changing my mind, and that if I get my way on this small point, I will sign the final papers.

It's blindingly bright in downtown Cedar Rapids. I feel like I'm coming outside into the sunshine after a long illness. My mother pulls the car onto a side street. There are a few oak trees, but there's nowhere to park in the shade.

When we get inside we find out that my social worker is on vacation. For a minute, I think I'm about to be swindled out of the visit with my baby. But another social worker, a woman, appears with the baby in her arms. This is the cutest baby I've ever seen. He has shiny hair that's almost black—like mine—and he has the sort of face that you'd see in a TV commercial. The people in the office are cooing over his long curling eyelashes. I'm sure they're thinking, "How can anyone give up a baby like this?" I can tell my mother is worrying about me and that everyone must know I'm the girl who is breaking the rules. I don't want to make a scene—I just want to hold my son.

The woman leads us past the desks and the cramped offices to an area with a couch and a changing table. She hands me a bottle and tells me I can feed him. My breasts begin to ache, and I remember the shot in the hospital that was supposed to dry up my milk. It occurs to me that perhaps it isn't working. The baby turns his head away as if to say this isn't working for him either. He's full-out wailing now, but my mother and I pass him back and forth, admiring him. He has all of his fingers and toes. He is beautiful and perfect.

My mother is mad at herself because she meant to bring a camera. She had it in her hands, she says, right before she walked out the door, but now it's not in her purse. I know how she is when she gets nervous. I imagine her checking for her cigarettes, her lighter, a pack of gum. Our minutes are ticking away, and there will be no record of them, but I think to myself that a photograph would be one more thing to hide. The social worker breezes back in with a diaper and says we can change the baby. After we finish with the diapering, she stands there, her arms outstretched. I know this is it—the final minute with my son.

I don't clutch my baby close to me. I don't kiss him. I hold him softly, the nubby texture of his yellow terry cloth suit against my hands and arms. And then I give him up without saying a word.

Dreaming as the Summers Die

Terri Elders

Still she haunts me, phantomwise

—Lewis Carroll

figured something special might be happening that July morning in 1948 when Mama appeared in the bedroom doorway, brandishing her boar-bristled hairbrush in one hand, my not-too-faded red plaid dress in the other.

"Skip the shorts and shirt today," she said, handing me the dress. "Company's coming for lunch."

"Who?" I asked, puzzled. I couldn't think of anybody important enough to wear my Sunday dress for, but I slipped into it and stood quietly while Mama tugged the brush through my snarls.

I had just turned eleven. No longer in pigtails, I hadn't yet mastered pin curls. So I wore my hair shoulder length and loose around my face, with bangs that forever needed trimming. Maybe I'd learn to set it with bobby pins before I started junior high that fall.

I waited for Mama to answer. "It's Nana," she finally said. "Nana, and maybe Jean." I looked up sharply. Jean was my "real" mother, and I hadn't seen her for years. I glanced across the bedroom at my older sister. Patti and I, just a year apart in age, had been adopted by our "real" father's sister and her husband in 1942, when we were five and six. Patti yawned, and then threw me a wink. Nearly a teen, she was more interested in boys than family gossip.

"Can I go over to Jimmy's?" I asked, as Mama patted my bangs into place.

"Okay. I'll send Patti over to get you when they get here. Just don't get too dirty."

Jimmy lived three doors down and was my best friend. The two of us would climb a towering maple tree to his roof where we would sit for hours, endlessly arguing. I favored the Brooklyn Dodgers and Doris Day. Jimmy loved the Giants and Peggy Lee. I liked Jack Benny, he Fred Allen. Though we rarely agreed, we relished our debates.

A few days earlier we had perched on the roof to watch the July 4 fireworks from the Los Angeles Coliseum. Some evenings we sat up there with Jimmy's telescope, searching for UFOs. We even argued about the merits of the planets. I preferred Jupiter, he Mars.

I'd be glad to see Nana, Jean's mother, who always wore sweet gardenia perfume and talked about how she conferred with spirits at her spiritualist church. But I barely remembered

Jean. I knew my Daddy Al, of course, Mama's brother, because he visited from time to time. Jean, though, was just a shadowy background figure, referred to in disapproving whispers. She drank, I'd heard. Or she had mental problems, whatever those might be.

She and Daddy Al had married when she was just a teenager, Mama said, and then Patti and I came quickly. Jean just couldn't manage.

More important to me, I knew she was the daughter of a world-famous organist, Jesse Crawford, known throughout the '30s as "The Poet of the Organ." Grandpa Crawford sent Christmas cards with photos. I'd heard that he'd had radio shows in Chicago, and was the featured performer at Radio City Music Hall in New York City. My sister had inherited all that musical talent, but none trickled down to me.

"Jean could have been a concert pianist," Mama said once. Jean's brother, Howard, was a musician, too. My taste in music ran more to Vaughn Monroe than classical. "Ballerina" was my current favorite. I'd hum it all the time, but wished I could play it on the upright. Not fair, I used to think. I was the one with the middle name, Jean, so I should be the one with the family talent.

Jimmy and I argued well past noon until Patti eventually appeared. "They're here," she announced, with a smirk and a roll of her eyes. I shinnied down the maple, careful not to tear my red plaid dress.

Jean looked younger than I expected, and prettier, with hair the same dark brown as mine, and freckles, just like mine, sprinkled across her nose. But during lunch she never smiled. Not once. Nana talked of the séances she conducted. Mama talked of how Patti and I soon would be starting junior high. Jean just sat, nibbled at her tuna sandwich, glanced about our tiny kitchen, and looked as bored as Patti.

I wanted to ask if she had seen *Easter Parade,* my new favorite movie. I wanted to ask where she lived, if she traveled, if she liked to play Parcheesi or Tripoley. I wanted to ask if she remembered when I was born. Which did she like to read, *Coronet* or *McCall's*?

But soon everybody was saying goodbye. Jean gave Patti and me each a hesitant hug. "You girls look great," she said, the first words she'd spoken directly to us all afternoon. I wanted to tell her that I liked her freckles, but before I could speak, they were all piling into Nana's Studebaker.

Later that summer, Jimmy's family moved away and I never saw him again. I never saw Jean again either. She just vanished. Nobody ever knew where she had gone. One afternoon a couple of years after that visit, I heard on the radio that my Nana, Olga Crawford, first wife of famed organist Jesse, had died in an apartment fire at the age of fifty-seven.

A few years later I sent for my birth certificate, which had been altered when I was adopted, to show Daddy and Mama as my parents. Astonished, I found my middle name was spelled Jeanne, not Jean. Was this how my "real" mother spelled it?

Grandpa Jesse came to my high school graduation and gave me a Smith Corona portable typewriter that I treasured all through college. Throughout the late '50s, I visited him frequently. He hadn't seen Jean since she was in her early teens and was uncertain about how her name was spelled.

I saw Daddy Al from time to time until he died in 1992. He had been married to Jean for such a brief time and so long ago. He had neither their wedding certificate nor divorce papers, so couldn't help me with the spelling.

Across the decades I think of her. Was she Jean or Jeanne? Did she read Hemingway or Fitzgerald? Would she choose pistachio or burgundy cherry if she were at Curries Ice Cream Parlor? Did she ever marry again or have more children? Do I have half-brothers or sisters that I don't know about?

Later, at UCLA, I spent a year interning for the Los Angeles County Department of Adoptions while I worked on a Master of Social Work degree. I learned about the adoption rules of earlier days, about sealed birth certificates and efforts to protect birth mothers. I also learned why many adult adoptees feel an urge to know, a need for answers.

Even now, in my seventies, I'd like to see my original birth certificate. Every time I sign my name, Theresa J. Elders, I wonder if that "J" stands for Jean or Jeanne. And I still dream about climbing maple trees…and about my mother's freckles.

The Lilac Bush

Kathe Kokolias

I am holding a lilac blossom in my hand. Lilac bushes are rare in this part of New York City. These lilacs cascade out of plastic vases and aluminum pails from a flower stand onto the sidewalk of Madison Avenue.

The lilac has hundreds of tiny individual flowers, each one complete in itself. Together they make up a delicate cluster of pale purple. I cup the blossom in both hands and bring it close to my face, inhaling the unmistakable, subtle fragrance that takes me back to my childhood home.

A lilac bush grew in our backyard, shaded by ancient oak trees. It was a scrawny, leggy plant that each year threatened to die but somehow rallied every May, producing blooms that lived gloriously but briefly. My mother sat in the backyard close to the lilac bush—a respite after scrubbing our house until her Spic and Span floors glistened. After wringing out the mop, she'd strip off her housedress and take a long bath, finishing off with a splash of Jean Naté Pour le Bain.

On warm late spring afternoons, she changed into cotton voile dresses of pale blue and green, but in my memory, she wears purple, like the blossoms she loved. I sit close to her, breathing in her fragrance mingled with the wafting aroma of lilacs. Her damp chestnut hair curls around her heart-shaped face. The deep brown eyes that my brother swore could see through the back of her head rest, unvigilant for the moment. All too soon it will be time to go back inside to start dinner and mix my father's Manhattan, ready to serve him when he walks through the door.

Years later, after I married and left home, my parents sold the house with the tenacious lilac bush and moved to Florida. For a while, their lives were filled with perpetual sunshine, their yard abundant with yellow hibiscus, pink bougainvillea and creamy gardenia that flourished year-round and seemed to thrive on neglect.

Although she never said it, I suspect that my mother believed she had a covenant with God, that if she was a good person, a dutiful wife, a respectful daughter, a loving mother, that she'd grow old and watch her grandchildren grow up. But it was a one-sided agreement. One spring just after Mother's Day, an unnamed illness struck her and gradually but relentlessly sapped her strength and her spirit. In the months that followed, I watched helplessly as her body failed to respond to the assault of various treatments. She surrendered the following winter, a few months after her fifty-seventh birthday, surrounded by flashy flowers that remained robust, inviolable, that did not know when to die—flowers that mocked my mother.

Here on a sidewalk in New York City, I hold a cool lilac lightly in my hand and bow my head to it. Its scent pierces my heart. I take in its sweetness, and the shady backyard of our house on Seventh Avenue, my mother in a purple voile dress seated next to the enduring lilac bush, once again heavy with bloom. Through a thin veil of Jean Naté tinged with Spic and Span, she opens her arms and gathers me in, welcoming me home.

We Are Gathered

Dianna Calareso

My dress hung in the hall closet, the closet that hid suitcases, old coats, Christmas decorations, and wrapping paper for every occasion. Simple, new, and black, it hung patiently until the week before, when the house exploded into madness. Papers and lists covered the dining room table like placemats. Response cards from people I didn't know filled the mailbox. Plane tickets, reservations, and order forms had taken the place of the report cards, coupons, and calendars that usually hung on the bulletin board. The menu was set, the guest list finalized, and appointments were made for the bridesmaids' pedicures. The last thing to be done was the program. As I looked over my mother's handwritten notes I saw that my cousin Lori was singing "Great Is Thy Faithfulness."

There was going to be a wedding. A big, beautiful wedding with dancing and food and laughter and tears over the marriage of the first daughter, my eldest sister, Marie. We all had a part: my other sisters, Susan and Annie, and I would stand as bridesmaids, Grandma would read a Psalm, and Lori would sing. Marie was scheduled to fly in from Los Angeles the first week of June. Even though she had established herself in California, my parents were adamant that the wedding would be in Florida where she was raised and people loved her. It didn't matter that people loved her in Los Angeles—Florida was where the family was.

I was brought up to understand that the sun and moon and stars revolved around the family. Not just our family, but the concept of something tight and bound and holding everything else in place: the nucleus of an atom, the stone of a peach, the palm of a hand. Even if parts fell away, if the atom spun or the peach was sliced or a finger was cut off like Grandpa's when he was intent on mastering the art of woodworking, the family would adjust, hold tighter, stand firmer. This wasn't just theory, either. This was knowledge passed down from years of braving the unpredictable climate of life, like our house in the hurricanes that barreled through every summer. Sometimes in these storms the palm trees lost their fronds and the black olive trees lost their thorny branches and we would go outside the next day, stomping through puddles and soggy grass, cleaning up what we could and leaving what we couldn't.

It was like that when Mom and Dad lost Anthony James, the brother I never knew, when Lori's brother Tony was killed as a teenager ten years ago, and finally in February when we laid to rest Grandpa, who didn't even remember that he was an Anthony—the first of the three born, the last to die.

—————

I was twelve years old when my mother hung up the phone, came into the family room, and said to my father, "Your nephew Tony is dead." I was sitting in a way that ordinarily my mother would have yelled at me for—on the arm of the easy chair, one leg draped over the side, most unladylike. But that day in July she didn't say anything, just stood with her wide green eyes filling up, her hand frozen over her mouth, her body rocking back and forth under her long robe. The rocking was something I got from her.

My dad and I got into the car with my suitcase. That day I was flying up to stay with my best friend's family at their cottage in Georgia, and though I was afraid that I wouldn't be able to go after the news of Tony, my dad told my mother to look for flights to Colorado and told me to get ready.

I sat alone in the front seat while my dad got out to pump the gas on the way to the airport. I tried to make myself cry. The fact that I wasn't already crying made me feel selfish and insensitive. I was sad, of course, but it was the sadness I felt when people died on TV—a brief reflection on what had happened, a passing thought about what I would feel like if that happened to me, but all this robed in the knowledge that it was somebody else's life and it was just make-believe. I wanted to cry for Tony, but he had always seemed more like Marie's cousin than mine because they were older than me. They had each other, and Susan and Lori had each other. My little sister Annie and I were usually assumed to be just fine by ourselves, even though every inch of me ached to be with the big kids. And by the time I was a big kid they had moved to Colorado.

"Do you have any questions? Anything you want to talk about?"

I thought for a minute. I was ashamed that the only thing I could think of was the Billy Joel song "Only the Good Die Young." I didn't even know how I knew it or where I had heard it, but it was spinning in my mind like the records I used to dig out of my dad's boxes in the garage, their cardboard covers dusty and swollen with humidity but the records as good as new on my old player. I didn't want to not ask anything, because this was one of those moments that only happened in movies when the parents let the kids ask anything they want. Usually we just took what my parents said as holy and immutable. Their traditional upbringings did not place kids and parents on a level playing field. As far as my parents were concerned, we were players and they were referees and coaches and if you questioned their authority you got a big fat penalty.

"Why do bad things happen to good people?" I knew he wouldn't have an answer to this question, any more so than if I had asked him to explain the meaning of life or my homework on photosynthesis. But if you get one free pitch you might as well throw the curve ball.

My father stumbled through an answer of how there was so much we didn't understand, but that God always had a reason for the things that happened and we just had to trust that this was all part of some greater plan. I pretty much knew this was going to be the answer, so while half of me listened to him the other half listened to Billy. At least *his* answer was decisive.

———∞∞∞———

I don't know if the news of Tony was easy to swallow because he seemed so far away, or because it was my second encounter with death. The first was the one I wasn't supposed to think about. It was the one I could never forget.

It was only two summers before, and we had gone up to Massachusetts to visit my parents' families. My parents had grown up in the Boston suburbs, but once they got married they said goodbye to winter and moved to Florida. It seemed that everyone who lived up there was one of my aunts or cousins, because my mother's father was one of ten children and all ten still lived in the area with their wives, children, and grandchildren. Only one of the ten never married—Aunt Maggie. She was a tall woman with big feet, a loud voice, and an effervescent way of telling stories that left us often entertained, sometimes confused, and always covered in spit that sprang from her flat bottom lip.

Aunt Maggie was in the process of opening a bed-and-breakfast in a beautiful old colonial home that she had renovated and restored and decorated with names of our family members in calligraphy on each of the guest room doors. She gave us a tour of the unfinished house, up the wide wooden staircase and down the narrow hallways and into the rooms. At each room she would stop and point out the elliptical hand-painted wooden nameplate, and my mother would say, "Oh, so-and-so, how is she?" or "Oh, so-and-so, such a lovely man." To most of these my sisters and I looked at each other, shrugged our shoulders, and giggled as our mother tried to interject comments into Aunt Maggie's stories.

We got to one of the last rooms on the hall and Aunt Maggie lightly touched the deep blue nameplate, looked at us, and said, "And this room is Anthony James, after your little brother."

"I don't have a brother," I replied quickly, scanning the faces of my mother and sisters to see if they all registered the same confusion. Only Annie's did. Susan and Marie looked at each other with "uh-oh-the-little-kids-just-found-out" expressions, and my mother looked at Aunt Maggie. She was speechless for the first time all day.

We stood on the big white porch of the house in the sunshine, Annie, my mother, and me, and as my mother spoke I looked down at my white beaded moccasins and tried to focus on how much I liked them rather than on how deceived I felt. My mother told us how her first child, born two years before Marie, had been a baby boy. They named him Anthony James, Anthony for my paternal grandfather and James for my maternal. He had lived less than a year. It wasn't until a few years later that I learned it was a liver disease that wouldn't have been a problem if he had been born ten years later. They had given him a full blood transfusion and tried everything, but it was the 1970s and so much hadn't been discovered yet.

When it was time to leave, my mother insisted that her four girls stand on the porch steps so she could take a picture. It came out nicely enough, my sisters and I smiling, my white moccasins and black and pink shirt the picture of coolness. But my smile was fake, and no amount of coolness could make up for the blow my young mind had taken. I was just so mad—mad that God would let a baby die, mad that something horrible had happened in my family, mad that I hadn't been in on the secret. And now I felt older, wiser in a way I didn't want to be wise. It was like all my life I had politely refused the fruit from the tree of good and evil and now somebody had shoved it down my throat. I had been allowed to know what the big kids knew, and now all I wanted was to not know anything. It was like when my best friend had told me about sex and my disgusted and confident reply had been, "Well *my* parents would never do *that!*"

The first time I ever mentioned Anthony James to my mother's mother, she was shocked that Mom hadn't told me. Then she was quiet for a moment and said gingerly, "That was such a sad time. The poor little thing just struggled and struggled."

———⟨φ/φ/φ⟩———

In seventh grade Mr. Jaswinski told us about an opportunity to submit original work to the upper school creative writing magazine, *Scribbler*. Mr. Jaswinski had been teaching English more years than I had been alive. He lectured in a monotone voice, paced four steps forward, rocked on his toe, then four steps backward, rocked on his heel, and so on. Every day, all class period. He didn't pronounce *h*'s at the beginning of words, so *humor* came out *yoomor* and *human* came out *yooman*. But he was so smart and so above us that more than anything I wanted to do well for him, to prove that I was smart and I understood his big words and his funny pronunciations.

The submissions could be any work of poetry, fiction, or nonfiction, and Mr. Jaswinski told us that we could use any of the creative writing assignments we had done in his class. I didn't have to think long. I would submit the only piece that I hadn't shown to my parents, the only piece I was proud to have earned a B+ on, the piece I had been afraid to write, afraid to hand in, and deathly afraid that Mr. Jaswinski would tell my parents about.

The assignment was "If one wish were granted to you, what would you ask for?" I thought for a long time before writing, not because I didn't know what I wanted, but because I was afraid to write it. I sat at my desk in my room staring at the notebook paper. I'd had the heading on for hours, my name, date, class period, and assignment. And then I remembered how deceived I had felt, how confused, how stifled. I remembered the first time I snooped through my mother's nightstand and found Anthony James's baby book, filled with pictures of a tan baby with dark eyes the color of wet firewood, and how every time I was home alone it pulled me like a magnet, and I sat on the floor of their room looking at the pictures until I heard the car pull up, shoved the book back in the nightstand, ran into my room, and closed the door quietly as if I'd been doing homework all along.

So I began to write. *Loving someone is hard when you've never met him or her. If one wish were granted to me, I'd wish I could meet my brother, Anthony James.* I erased and then rewrote his name, and decided if I was going to write this for real then I would have to write it all. I wrote his real name, assured that I would love my brother as a friend, promised that I would tell him how much I appreciated him, and almost cried as I wrote the final line: *Nevertheless, I do not worry about him because I know he is safe and happy in Heaven where God has been taking care of him since he was a baby.* It was done, and I was at the same time both proud of my work and ashamed.

A month later the stacks of *Scribbler* were delivered to all the English classes. Each student received a copy, whether or not he or she had submitted. I turned to the table of contents and there it was: *I'd Be Pleased to Meet You, by Dianna Calareso...pg. 7.* I was elated to be a published author, but my elation quickly turned to fear when I realized what I'd done. This had my name on it, my family's name on it, my dead brother's name on it. It was a sweet reflection of a sad memory, a memory my parents had never given me any authority to share.

I didn't say anything to my parents when I got home, and they said little to me. They had to know. Thankfully Marie was already off at college, but Susan would have received a copy. I hadn't told her about my submission, and I didn't know if I could trust her not to show it to Mom and Dad. She had been the one who told my mother when I said "sucks" on the school bus in kindergarten, not because I knew what it meant but because all the older kids were saying it. She was the one who had blurted out at the dinner table, "Your hair looks red!" when my parents hadn't noticed that Marie and her friend had dyed my hair maroon because they thought it would be fun and I would do anything for their approval.

A couple days later I noticed a copy of *Scribbler* in the basket behind the couch, the basket for old magazines and catalogs that were saved but never looked at again. Eventually it was covered under a new pile of old magazines; I never looked for it, and I never took my copy out of my backpack.

I didn't think about Tony again until Grandpa's memorial service. This death didn't just make me feel older, like the others had. This one made me feel like I had finally closed the door of innocence behind me, not because I wanted to but because somebody had pushed me through. I was twenty-one and this death seemed to seal off my childhood.

Childhood was agreeing to let Grandpa hold me on his shoulders to help decorate the Christmas tree, screaming when he promised he would only look at my loose tooth but yanked it out with a single pull, riding on the back of his motorcycle with my arms squeezing into his belly and my hair flying out from the special red helmet he bought for the kids. Adolescence was spending the last two summers getting acquainted with Alzheimer's, driving Grandma and him to doctors' appointments so that I could sit with him in the waiting room and assure him that she was coming back, watching him in the rearview mirror on the way home from his cataract surgery as he talked to a little boy he swore was in the car, marveling that in spite of everything he forgot he always remembered how to hold a banana like a phone so we could have our pretend conversations in the house. Adulthood was putting it all to rest.

My father asked my sisters and me if we wanted to write something to read at the service, if we thought we could get through without crying. I said I'd be okay, since this was one of those times we were supposed to be glad it was finally over, that he was no longer suffering, that he had a new mind and a new body in Heaven. These were things I could say so I wouldn't have to admit that really I was selfish because I wanted him back, broken mind and all. I sat on my bed with a notebook and tried to think of what I could say that would make people see how much he had meant to me.

I had achieved that at school—I devoted my senior year of college to writing a one-act play about the previous summer with him. The play was read by a group of student actors to an audience of twenty on February seventeenth; on February eighteenth he was gone. I was stunned by the timing, shocked that he could have left me like this, the same way I felt when I was seven and Mom dropped Annie and me off at a piano lesson that we didn't actually have that day, and we rang the doorbell and banged on the windows and finally sat on the edge of the driveway and cried because we felt like orphans.

I wondered what they had said at Tony and Anthony

James's memorial services. At least with Grandpa you could say he was better off, with no more long days of lethargy, confusion, anxiety, and nightmares keeping both him and my grandmother awake. But with a sixteen-year-old you couldn't say it was better, especially since Tony was killed in an accident that was never explained to me. And with an infant you couldn't say it was better, since he never really lived before he died. Grandpa was the only Anthony to make it this far, and I wondered if the three of them were finally getting to do all the things they never could as boys with their grandfather. I wondered if they would laugh with delight if someone called out "Tony!" and they all turned around.

At the service Susan, Annie, and I sat close together behind Marie and her fiancée. The chapel was small, the Marines that came to honor Grandpa were young and crisp, and the pew was littered with tissues. Susan spoke first and recited words from a song about Heaven. Marie talked about memories she and Tony had shared with Grandpa, like breaking down in his car and stealing pudding pops from his freezer. She told him to give Tony a hug for her. Annie talked about how she walked like Grandpa, and how what he loved most were hot French fries, pretty girls, and baseball. I talked about the one-act play and how finally he would get to see the two grandsons named for him.

The whole time I watched Grandma, trying to be strong and barely crying, my father, catching his tears before they fell, and my mother. She and I were both rocking back and forth as if in rhythm to our grief.

I used to imagine horrible scenarios of my parents dying

in car accidents and moving off to live with my mother's sister and her children. I imagined our new life with new parents. What scared me the most was how sometimes these thoughts seemed exciting—a new home, a new school. And then I would think more clearly and want to wipe my mind clean like an Etch-A-Sketch.

—⁙—

I was amazed at how hard it was to give my speech at the service, how easy it was later to block the whole ordeal out of my mind when I was busy, how paralyzing the grief was when it came suddenly and all I could do was freeze and wait for it to overtake me like a tidal wave. In these moments I ached. My chest hurt from trying to hold still a heart that yearned to find its missing piece. I was inconsolable, frustrated at my weakness and the mess I made of myself as my eyes and nose ran furiously and my head throbbed from violent sobs. I had always been one to "get over it," but now I faced a death that wouldn't leave me alone.

I understood, then, why Anthony James was such a family secret. It wasn't anything to be ashamed of—it was something that would come back and sting often enough without the encouragement of storytelling. My mother's grief had never left her. I discovered this when she read me a poem she had written about Anthony James called "Hope Deferred." She had assigned her eighth-grade students to write a poem, then decided to take on the assignment herself. She read it to me with clarity, poise, and the peaceful expression of one who has accepted the past and moved on, but when she got to the last line she lost it. I don't remember a single word of the poem because of how suddenly all the words were swallowed up in her tears. She sobbed right there in front of me, the paper shaking in her hand, her face distorted. I didn't know what to do so I put my arm around her and gently rocked her as she cried, shocked at how suddenly this storm had hit her, terrified at the power it had to break her down in an instant.

I also understood why it had taken almost ten years for my aunt and uncle to clean out Tony's room, the bed still unmade and clothes from that day still draped on the desk chair, his suitcase half-packed with things he was preparing to take to band camp. All I had been told was that he had gone outside, and after a while my aunt went to look for him and found him shot dead. Nobody saw it coming. His room was just as any sixteen-year-old boy's would have been on any normal day. I imagined the room covered in dust like an ancient castle, mildew climbing the walls and everything smelling like Tony and dirty clothes. I imagined the smell of him building up in the room like a fog, his parents too afraid to open the door and let it seep out. Every day would remind them he was gone, and even when it started getting easier there were always the sneak attacks. No use squandering a day of peace by going into his bedroom.

⎯⎯⎯⎯⎯⎯ a/a/a ⎯⎯⎯⎯⎯⎯

I liked the idea of Lori singing "Great Is Thy Faithfulness" at the wedding. It was one of the hymns my mother used to sing Marie to sleep when she was a baby. I remembered hearing "Trust and Obey" when she sang to Annie and me together in the room with the bunk beds. I had used these songs when I started babysitting, rocking infants against my chest and rubbing their soft warm backs as I sang. If I could feel this much love for a baby that wasn't mine, my mother's heart must have overflowed onto the floors of our nurseries as she sang to us; it must have clenched like a fist when she knew she would no longer sing to Anthony James. But the songs were hopeful, and a wedding was a commitment to the future. I imagined that when my mother heard the song she would no longer be watching a woman in a white dress, but a tiny child, the baby that had restored hope to a mother's broken heart.

I tried to imagine how my father and his brother would feel—they had each lost a son and a father—and realized I knew. They were desperate to cling to what they had, wives and daughters and a mother who cried by herself because when she was with people she felt she should laugh. I knew they felt this way by the daily phone calls, emails, and constant affirmation that we were loved and special. We were special because we had lived. We had life with promise and hope, promise and hope painfully lost in others along the way. We were a family. And I realized that even if the grief never stopped visiting like a ghost in a hooded cape, it would always be just that: a visitor. Death had aged us, but it had not killed us, and our only choice was to live. And on this day, we would celebrate.

Finding the Words

Maria Duffy

squeezed my husband's hand tightly. I couldn't bear to look at his face, usually so cheerful but now etched with pain as he sat by his fading dad's bedside. His mum too looked broken. The heartbreak of losing her partner of fifty years glistened in her eyes. The last moments were excruciating. The room heaved with grief as the family said their final goodbyes.

We sat outside the room afterward, each lost in our own thoughts. The silence was broken only by the soft sound of sobs. It seemed as though the moment had been frozen, as though everything had stopped in honor of his death.

Although we knew he'd passed, it felt strange waiting for the doctor to officially pronounce my father-in-law dead. It was as though a little part of us thought she might say it hadn't happened. Given the intensity of the situation, nothing seemed impossible. The doctor's next words didn't help. She emerged

95

from the room, head bowed respectfully, and said, "I'm sorry to have to tell you that your father...your husband...has passed away." Then she added, "For the moment."

I stifled a giggle. It was wholly inappropriate to laugh at a time like this, but it wasn't out of disrespect or lack of sadness. It just seemed like a particularly odd thing for her to say.

My next thought was my children. How was I going to tell them that their beloved granddad had died? They knew he was sick and we'd forewarned them that he wasn't going to get better. But to my four-year-old, "sick" was when he was home from playschool with a pain in his tummy and "really sick" was when Liam Delaney threw up three times into the bin in the classroom. How would I translate "sick" into "dead"?

There was no avoiding it. The children would be home from school soon and I needed to be there. I headed down to the car-park, leaving my husband to grieve with his family. Robbie Williams' "Angels" was playing on the radio. I turned the volume to the highest setting and finally let the tears flow. Alone in the sanctuary of the car I didn't have to be strong. It had been awful to see my husband fall apart at the loss of his dad. I'd always felt lucky and protected, but now the sheer vulnerability of life scared me.

My two oldest children cried immediately on hearing the news. The younger ones took a little longer but they soon sobbed along with the rest of us. It's not that they didn't care as much, but at four and six they were finding it harder to understand.

The family decided to celebrate my father-in-law's life by bringing him home to a traditional Irish wake. It was exactly what he would have wanted. He was placed in the sitting room in an open coffin and would remain there overnight. Prayers would be said and people could come and go to pay their respects. Never having experienced such an event, I was daunted. I thought it would be scary and devastatingly sad.

In fact, it was quite the opposite. Although there were plenty of tears, there was also a feeling of calmness and love. It lifted our hearts to see so many people pass through the house, each with their own story to tell. He would have loved it.

I couldn't make up my mind whether I should let my children see their granddad in his coffin. I hadn't seen a dead person when I was a child and I wondered if it would scare them out of their wits. Deciding to let them make up their own minds, I brought them to the house but sidestepped them into the kitchen.

"Listen," I said. "Granddad is in there in his coffin but you might not want to see him. If you like, you can just remember him in your head the way he used to be."

All four of them wanted to see him. So, one by one, I brought them in. My older son went right up to him and broke down. He said it didn't look like Granddad. My ten-year-old daughter got as far as the door and that was enough. The six-year-old girl ventured right up to the coffin and even managed to touch his hand.

But it was my four-year-old son who stunned us all. He bravely went into the room, where people sat with their well-fingered beads reciting the rosary. He went up to his granddad's face and touched it. He took a walk around the coffin, taking in everything. He was only short of getting in himself, such was his curiosity.

I wanted to make sure he understood what he saw so I brought him back to the crowded kitchen for a chat. How do you explain something like that to a four-year-old when it's difficult enough to understand ourselves?

"How do you feel after seeing your granddad in his coffin?" I asked, kneeling down beside him.

"Okay," he said. He didn't seem too fazed.

"Darling, you know Granddad won't wake up again, don't you?"

"Mam," he said, "is it like this?" He looked at me with big, honest eyes. "The granddad we knew isn't here anymore. The granddad who laughed and teased us, who tickled us and played with us is gone up like a shadow to Heaven. What's in that coffin is just a shell of his body so that we can remember what he looked like."

I couldn't believe it. My baby son had just uttered the words I'd been so desperately trying to find. How could he be so clever at just four years old? I fought hard to swallow the lump that formed in my throat and squeezed him tightly.

"Yes, darling. That's exactly right."

"I thought so," he said, skipping off to grab a piece of cake. "I saw it on *The Simpsons*."

This time there was no holding back the laughter. I was reminded of a quote I once heard: "We worry about what a child will become tomorrow, yet we forget that he is someone today." I'll never underestimate my children again.

The Santa Sack

Glynis Scrivens

I didn't cry until you quietly handed me your Santa sack.

"I guess I won't be needing this anymore," you said. Neither of us had realized until this moment that we were saying goodbye. We had been too busy.

Not a French *au revoir*, although naturally we'd still be seeing each other, probably every week. No doubt at dinnertime.

And of course, not an *adieu*. Nothing so final.

Perhaps something in between?

Is there a word adequate enough for this leave taking? The letting go of childhood and the reaching out to something new, just beyond the horizon?

I fingered the soft cotton pillowslip I had sewn twenty-four years ago. Only a few months ago I had filled it, knowing it would be for the last time. Suddenly your needs were for adult things. A recipe book. A blender. Tea towels. Cutlery. It had felt strange putting it under our Christmas tree. It felt like a contradiction to put such practical items into the very same pillowslip that had held your Lego kits and skateboard. We were playacting this time, holding onto a past we knew had already slipped through our fingers.

Of course, love never slips through fingers. And somehow this pillowslip epitomized that. It wasn't perfect, far from it. But it was durable. There was a sameness that made it irreplaceable, even when we could have afforded something better. Even when your kite split a whole side seam one year, I simply mended it. Throwing it out was unthinkable.

Before handing it to me, you gave it one last sniff, holding it to your face and inhaling deeply. "I love this smell," you said. "It's always been very special." And you confided that each Christmas as you had sat up quietly in bed as a young boy, exploring the contents of your Santa sack in the dark, you had first paused to breathe in its magic.

I close my eyes and breathe in. But it's not magic I find. It's love. The pillowslip smells of you.

And yet to an outsider, it's simply a faded homemade Santa sack, sewn from cheap fabric. I had found the remnant of green cotton at a post-Christmas sale. The cheeky Santas on it won me over. I was pregnant, and wondered whether it would make a cool pair of rompers, or maybe a dress if my baby was a girl. Everything lay ahead of me that day as I held the fabric.

Where have those years gone?

Have I really hidden gifts in this slip twenty-four times?

It doesn't seem possible. Yet here you are in front of me, a young adult, leaving home to start a new phase of your life. A life where childhood things like a Santa sack and a teddy bear would take up space needed for the new life you're embarking on. It's not that you don't hold them dear. It's that you fear they will hold you back.

When I was a very young child, my mother made reins for us—something to make sure we stayed by her side on those trips into the city. She didn't have enough hands to hold onto each one of us, so this seemed the only way she could show the city sights to her curious young brood. I have no memory of wearing the reins now, just the occasional reminder of them in photos.

But I clearly remember the excitement of those trips, of being introduced to department stores, of eating new foods such as fruit mince pies and tropical fruit sundaes. Of frosted caramels, bustling crowds, noise, trams. The highlight each year was the brilliant Christmas displays, when shop windows would be transformed by moving characters re-enacting nursery rhymes.

The Santa sack is also a set of reins. Something to hold you to me, keep you within the safe loving circle of family. A rein of tradition and family rites. Yet as you grow older, they are replaced by invisible ties—bonds of love that mature into respect, consideration, sometimes even awe. It's these invisible ones that last. We can let go of the others.

Blinking back tears, I carefully lay the pillowslip in the bottom drawer of my dressing table, beside an ancient pair of reins.

101

A Tree of Life

Amy Munnell

 was eleven when I learned that children die. My sister taught me three months before her thirteenth birthday.

Marcia's life stopped short of the things that make living an adventure: the embarrassment of puppy love, the humor in hangovers, the pomp of graduation, and first encounters with shades of gray. She never grew up so I did.

Only eighteen months apart, Marcia and I shared an important trait. Spinal Muscular Atrophy put us on wheels from the start. Numbers four and five out of eight kids, our parents raised us to be as normal as possible out of necessity. Since Marcia was older, she became the guinea pig. I just followed in her tracks.

On my mother's insistence, we were mainstreamed into the public school system before anyone put the words "politically" and "correct" together. For most of our childhood, we knew no other disabled children.

When Marcia moved from grade school to middle school, our parents got nervous. In elementary school, they dropped her off at her desk in the morning and picked her up right there at 2:30 each afternoon. Students moved from room to room in middle school. Marcia pushed her chair at a snail's pace. How would she keep up?

"Becky will be in some of my classes," Marcia explained. Her best friend often pushed her chair for her. "The teachers will help find someone heading to my next class." To both of us, it was simple, and finally she reassured our parents.

Marcia did fine getting from class to class, just as she said she would, but each winter brought chest colds and the flu, challenging her fragile health. Just after Christmas in 1973, she caught a cold.

"Don't tell," she begged our sister Emily while getting dressed one morning. "I don't want to stay home." Emily promised not to, but the cold turned out to be the flu and in a matter of weeks it became pneumonia. Our parents banned me from her bedroom to keep me from getting sick.

"Whatcha watching?" I asked every afternoon, parking my chair in the doorway. The doorway was not the bedroom, we rationalized.

"Gilligan," she replied. "You missed Andy Griffith. It was the one when Gomer was deputized. 'Citizens a-rest! Citizens a-rest!'"

We talked through the crack between the door and doorjamb, my chair blocking most of the doorway. Sometimes Matt, Mandy, and Clayton, our younger siblings, squeezed past to sit on the floor in front of the TV.

I didn't know that she was dying and can't say if she knew or not. We didn't talk about it. We simply watched 1960s sitcom reruns.

I knew she had died before the ambulance left the house that March morning. Daddy's heavy footsteps carried her to their bed as Mom made a panicked call for the ambulance. Then she counted the one-two-three-four-five-breathe rhythm of CPR.

I didn't cry then or when they came home without her or even at the memorial service, surrounded by a church full of people. They had all been touched by my sister, touched so deeply as to sit through the "March of the Siamese Children" and "On Top of the World," music my mother chose, and through a sermon by a minister who had never met her.

I did cry that night, hiding my face with my arm. Daddy sat on the bed and rubbed my back. He said I could talk about it, but I shook my head, embarrassed to admit I was a brat. I thought of last summer when we had fought over my watercolor paints.

"But you have the palette thing and that thin brush," she whined.

"So what?" I shouted, pushing mine deeper inside my desk. She had her own, she didn't need mine.

I wasn't like her, and no matter how hard I tried, I'd never be her. Even her friends looked for her inside me, coming over even though we had rarely played together before. I always disappointed them. Marcia left me alone in a spotlight I didn't want.

My eyes still swell at that spotlight, the sudden apple of my dad's eye. Anything I needed or wanted he gave to me. I was his shield against the guilt spawned by the loss of his child and a large brick in the wall that rose between him and my mother.

Outside the family, in school and beyond, I had to be the one to open the doors, to prove what a person in a wheelchair could do, to be the first in line, front and center, by myself. As I moved to middle school to high school to college, my coping skills often fell short of the challenges, turning me inside.

Nothing could replace the loss of Marcia from my life, or fill the void growing deep within me. I met other disabled students in college and happily stepped aside for them to lead, but it wasn't the same. They didn't know me, nor would I let them know me. I wasn't like them. I wouldn't let myself be.

How would life have been different if she had lived? How would I have been? Would we have been best friends? Would I have taken more chances? I lost so much without really knowing what I had.

Then one spring my nieces and nephews climbed the cherry tree outside my window. We had planted it with Marcia's ashes. I watched, forgetting the deadline written in red on my calendar, ignoring my computer, the phone. When they noticed me, they waved through showers of pink petals.

Mom didn't like them climbing that tree, but I liked it. I liked it a lot. They laughed as they hugged the limbs, feeling its life, their own lives, maybe even Marcia's life, through the bark of this memorial. They competed to climb higher, but usually found contentment sitting in the V of the thickest branches.

More than thirty years have passed since her death. My nephews and nieces, now college students, no longer climb her branches, but Marcia blooms with the daffodils each year. The squirrels play on her limbs, raiding the bird feeders. Wrens nest in the tiny houses. A falcon has roosted there, puffed up against a summer rain. Her leaves turn yellow-gold in the fall, and her branches bend in a sudden winter ice storm.

That vast hole remains inside me, swirling with questions and doubts. When I find myself sliding into it, I forget everything else and watch Marcia's tree outside my window. Among the sorrow and confusion at the hole's bottom lie the barely-pink blossoms of spring to cushion my fall.

At Gilda's

Jennifer Lang

ow your chin to your chest and thank your bodies for their strength and cooperation," I say to my students at the end of every yoga class. With my eyes still closed, I think about the people sitting on their mats in front of me. I wonder what these words mean to them. Here, at Gilda's Club, all my students have some intimate connection to cancer. They might be undergoing treatment, in remission, or living with a loved one who has cancer.

"I've just finished chemotherapy and am feeling okay enough to be here," Charlotte had said, introducing herself before her first class. An older woman with a brassy red wig and splotches of blush on her cheeks, she moved slowly. "I used to do yoga but am having trouble feeling my feet on the floor lately."

Rich waited patiently for Charlotte to finish talking. A newcomer to Gilda's, he was the only male I had seen on the premises since I'd started teaching there six months earlier. The subject of kids came up, and he mentioned his own. As soon as I looked him in the eyes, I felt the hair on my arms stand on end. Short and muscular, Rich wore a gold wedding band on his left ring finger. He looked about what my husband and I call "our" age. In Rich, I saw my spouse, my friends' spouses, our peers.

Another new woman, Diana, took me aside. "Ever since the cancer I've developed lymphedema," she said quietly. I had no idea what that meant. Wearing a sky blue paisley scarf wrapped tightly around her head, Diana had dark sunken eyes. She also looked my age—late thirties, early forties. "That's why I wear this brace and can't bear any weight on my left arm. It's because of the cancer, you know?" I didn't. Still, I listened. I told her to do what she could, to respect her body.

⸻ ✦ ✦ ✦ ⸻

Gilda's Club Westchester came into my life via email: "Anyone interested in teaching yoga to people whose lives have been touched by cancer, please call." Intrigued, I set up an interview.

"Have you had contact with people who've had cancer?" a social worker asked as soon as we sat down. I nodded. It seemed like the disease had been ever-present in my life. I knew a lot of people who had survived, but mostly I thought of those who hadn't. In third grade, my friend Karen's mom had died of uterine cancer. Throughout high school, my friend Kim was in and out of treatment for Hodgkin's lym-

110

phoma. In my mid-twenties, my mom's best friend died of complications from breast cancer. Then there was my old classmate Annie whom I hadn't seen in almost twenty years. Weeks before this interview, I had learned from my mom that she'd been diagnosed with ovarian cancer at age thirty-seven.

I shared some of these stories with the social worker. I confessed my desire to confront it—my fears, my own mortality.

And I got the job.

When family or friends asked why I wanted to volunteer there, I found it difficult to explain. Secretly, I hoped that by teaching at Gilda's Club, in confronting cancer like this, maybe I could protect myself. I couldn't even finish the thought, to face the fact that I could fall prey to a deadly diagnosis. Just like Annie. I couldn't share the fear about my mortality that had haunted me ever since my own near-collision with death.

Rich became one of the regulars at Gilda's. He was there every time I taught, pushing his body through poses.

"I'm really angry about the brain tumor," he told me just before his second class. "I was talking with another woman who has one and she said yoga can help with anger." I studied him. I saw his pained expression, sensed his vulnerability. With a chic bandana across his forehead and the top of his skull, he resembled a guy in a Gap ad. "What do you think?" he asked.

"Well," I began, choosing my words carefully. I didn't

know where to begin or how I would stop. "That might be. I don't know if it's true for everyone, but I know for me it helped a lot." And then I opened up to him—something I hadn't yet done with the others. I told him about my own physical ordeal two years earlier.

Late that March, toward the end of a two-hundred-hour intensive yoga teacher training program, I had developed a physical strength that was totally foreign. In fact, strong was the last word I would have ever used to describe my five-foot frame. But after six months of daily yoga, assisting my peers in different poses and learning various techniques to control my breath, I felt full of vigor. I thought I could breathe my way through life.

One week after the program had ended, on an exceptionally cold April night, a wave of knife-shooting pain pierced my abdomen. My body fell out from under me. Throughout the following two weeks, as I battled with debilitating abdominal pain, I sought help, went to yoga and carpooled my kids to school. Mostly, though, I breathed deeply. Friends and family told me I looked pale. Unconvinced, I reassured them I would be fine. After a second fainting spell, my doctor finally determined it was an IUD-related ectopic pregnancy and sent me directly to the ER for surgery.

When the medical staff attached an oxygen tube under my nose and an IV in my arm, I shook with fear. I suddenly realized we cannot always control our bodies. Physically, I had felt stronger than ever, but strength had nothing to do with it. I was wheeled away on a gurney to remove a ruptured fallopian tube and receive a life-saving blood transfusion.

I told Rich I was lucky to be alive, but I didn't really feel lucky. Instead, I felt as if someone had opened up my body and physically removed my muscles. Before the operation, I could gracefully swing my legs up into a handstand; after, I couldn't even sit up in my hospital bed.

During my recovery, I was consumed by anger toward my body's failure to protect me and the doctors' delayed diagnosis. I searched for someone to take the blame—the company that made the contraceptive device, the FDA, the doctor. I started thinking in before-surgery and after-surgery terms. Nothing had prepared me to face my own mortality.

Rich listened attentively to my story, nodding his head. When the doctor told me my incision looked beautiful and was fully healed six weeks later, I hesitantly got back on my yoga mat. Void of strength or stamina and scared that anything strenuous, twisted or upside down would tear my incision, I took gentle classes—for beginners, the infirm, the aged. As the weeks passed, I slowly let the yoga in and began to trust my body again. I felt the floor underneath my feet and the beautiful dance of my breath with movement.

Ever since Rich and I met, I have waited anxiously to see if he would come to class each week. I wanted to know he was okay. That he would survive.

✦✦✦

Then there's Annie. Whenever I'm at Gilda's Club, I think of her. I picture her the way I remember her from high school, with sun-bleached hair and muscular upper arms

113

from being on the swim team. Whenever she smiled, her whole face lit up. It was as if all the exposure to sun made her glow.

Annie and I had gone to the doctor with the same symptoms. Yet it had never occurred to me that my unbearable abdominal pains could be cancer. And I couldn't imagine what it would be like to be her or Rich or anyone else in the prime of life, dealing with a potential death sentence. How could they ever make sense of what was happening? Had Annie been angry, like Rich, or accepting? Did she have cancer because she was strong enough somehow to handle it in a way that others, like me, were not? I knew my thoughts were wholly irrational. Life—illness, health, death—doesn't work like that.

My mom called. A year and a half after her diagnosis, Annie passed away. She died at the age of thirty-eight, leaving behind a husband and two young children, around the same ages as mine. I shudder knowing that she will not be able to watch them grow up. They will never know how exquisite their mother was.

⸺⊱⊰⸺

I watch my students—Charlotte, Diana, Rich—during *shavasana*, corpse pose, at the end of class this time. Usually, I turn away, guiding them into the final resting pose with their backs flat on the mats, arms outstretched by their sides, eyes shut, and then close my eyes for five minutes to give them privacy. Now I look. And I see them not as students but as survivors, each of whom, like me, have a before and after point of reference. They know what it is to have their bodies betray them. And I recognize that while my near-death experience with the IUD was hard, it is over. For my students it's different. They will live with their disease for the rest of their lives.

In the final minutes of class, we sit up facing each other, our eyes closed. I feel tears begin to burn. At my edge emotionally, I realize what I am asking of my students, acknowledge the weight of my words: "Thank your bodies for their strength and cooperation." They might not be able to do either. They can't know what their futures hold or if they or their loved ones will be able to live with the disease.

As my students and I bow our chins to our chests, I think about Annie again. I realize that young or old, strong or weak, we are all vulnerable. I truly understand what I have been hearing my yoga teachers say over the years. We are simply given these bodies to dwell in while we are here. They are only temporary. All we can do is listen to them and care for them.

Ghosthouse

Roberta Beach Jacobson

M y husband was eager to see my old northern Illinois neighborhood, and due to a freak spring storm we had the chance to view my childhood home decorated in snow. We had a camera with us, but there was simply no shuttered house to photograph.

I couldn't understand it. I turned the car around at the next corner and tried again.

"Are you sure you remember the number right?" he asked.

I considered Alf's question carefully. The tree-lined street was only five blocks long. I knew where I once lived and was absolutely sure the number was five-oh-one. In fact, I was with my dad when he bought the metal numbers at the hardware store and affixed them to the garage. Besides that, every morning and afternoon I'd walked the family poodle and I knew every crack in the sidewalk, every neighbor, every house on the street. Both sides of the street. I sold Girl Scout cookies on that street. I trick-or-treated on that street.

I could feel a trickle of sweat on my cheek. We had the camera out of the case and were driving exactly where we should be. The street sign verified it. I had no plausible explanation for my husband. Or for myself. Something was amiss. The house was gone, but that defied logic.

I suspected my husband was under the impression his wife had lost a few marbles. What sort of woman insists her new spouse travel for hours to photograph her former home, but then is unable to locate it?

We returned the rental car and I did my best to explain the situation to my mother, who was eager for news on how the old neighborhood looked. "I know it sounds spooky, Mom, but the house seems to have disappeared," I told her.

She suggested somebody must have painted the exterior or removed the shutters and I just didn't recognize the house as we drove by. I didn't buy a word of it. The house had vanished!

How the house disappeared remained a mystery. I considered it an unfinished chapter in my life and pondered it from time to time. For years, no explanations appeared to comfort me. Then one Christmas, out of the blue, a neighbor from days long past sent me a cheery card with a note. She told me how the next-door neighbors (five-oh-three) had purchased our former property and had our house knocked down. They needed to extend their house for grandkids' visits.

Once I let out my tears, gales of laughter followed. I'd

rented a car only to drive Alf to a ghosthouse!

I pondered how new generations would form their own childhood memories in the same spot I grew up—climbing trees, walking Grandpa's dog, raking leaves, shoveling snow.

All that's left of my childhood home is a box of photos. A wrecking ball took away the walls and windows with green shutters. Digging machines removed the patio and the wooden fence. I have my five-oh-one memories, and now it's time for me to allow others the time and space to create theirs.

Pickles

Gail Kirkpatrick

After my mother passed away, my sister and I cleaned out her apartment. We worked in sisterly companionship, following Mom's wishes to "keep what is needed and give the rest to charity." It wasn't easy going through her personal belongings—pawing through drawers, folding up the sheets from her bed, removing items from a laundry hamper, moving furniture. We couldn't help but feel like intruders. Aside from our sorrow, our respect for her personal space remained, and a kind of reverence impeded. Nevertheless, my sister and I did the best we could.

The woman we knew was illuminated in a neatly folded pile of never-worn scarves, pictures tucked into the frames of larger photos, notes on family ancestry labeled "important papers." Behind the stove, Debbie found a packet of matches from their Hawaii trip, and in the hall closet, I found a bag of pictures of my grandfather in his coffin that my mother had never gotten around to throwing away. Neighbors stopped by to express their sympathy. The day proceeded in quiet efficiency. After all, we had learned the art of cleaning from an expert.

We stopped for a break and decided to help ourselves to the rye in the freezer. When we opened the refrigerator to look for Pepsi, we found sixteen jars of homemade dill pickles.

Our mother may have told us that she was making pickles, but in the light of life-altering challenges, it must not have meant much to us at the time. Between the hours of waiting for the chemo to drip into her veins, distracting trips to the casino the day after, trying to act as if normal life was carrying on, we took no notice of what she might be doing in her apartment on her own. Yet, there in the back the cold jars of dills were waiting. Their green was still evolving from the color of crisp young cucumbers to fully pickled ones. Shiny, incisor-sized garlic pieces had settled to the bottom, and dill weed was suspended in the preserving sea.

What bewildered me most was trying to understand why someone who may be facing the end of her days on earth would spend her time making pickles. People take trips to dreamed-of Shangri-Las or buy the car they have always wanted to drive. Why would they make pickles?

My mother was born in a log house. The prairie was her playground. She went to Christmas concerts in a horse-drawn sleigh with a warmed stone at her feet. I have a picture of her holding a guitar, but she never plucked a string in my lifetime. She insisted on finishing high school when her parents thought she had had more than enough education. It was the late 1940s. She trained as a psych nurse, but the one mark she needed to meet the standards no one would give. We assumed she was happiest hoeing potatoes and pinching pierogies. She knit sweaters for her grandchildren, and when they were ill, her arthritic fingers curled around her rosary.

My father was a railway agent and we lived in a Canadian National railway station. Mom and Dad talked about owning a house someday, but when he passed away, she moved from apartment to apartment. She followed her grandchildren to the West Coast, and in her twice-daily walks along the water, she looked east. When her brother left her some money, she was able twice yearly to fly over the Rockies back to the wheat fields.

⟞◦◦◦⟝

It now makes complete sense. The only thing that she would want to do, while she had the strength, was that which brought her simple, sensory joy. She needed to practice the memory of what she had spent a lifetime doing. It must have been a kind of gift to herself in a way that maybe even she didn't fully understand—a gift of the familiar, the earthly, the spiritual. Remembering what it was like in her railway garden, picking fresh morning cucumbers, scrubbing them in cool water, getting the correct proportions of salt and vinegar, inhaling the steaming brine and the scent of dill weed.

Placing the garlic into the bottom of the jar and the dill alongside, and then pushing the cucumbers tightly together in the jars, and canning them to make sure everything was sealed.

It was deliberate, joyful labor with productive outcome. No miracles to pray for, the results known, felt in her bones. Was she also secretly celebrating that in the future, the pickles would be found, opened, and in their salty crunch, she would have never passed away?

The apartment cleaned, we divided the jars. I still have one on display on a shelf, never to be opened. I think about all of these things as I stand packing dills into jars.

Memorial Day

Deanna Hershiser

HELLO AGAIN, COAST

indows open to salty breezes, we drive uphill at the west end of town. My husband, Tim, steers us toward the beach road.

We're here, the Friday of Memorial Day weekend, because our son needs to rendezvous with his marine biology class at an Oregon coast tide pool tomorrow morning. We decided to make the two-hour trip from our Willamette Valley home and camp tonight. Tim used to be an engineer for the local TV station—he helped maintain an array of nearby transmitters and towers. As he tells our son stories of gale force storms and equipment failures, I glance at passing landmarks.

An unexpected shudder threads up my spine. Should I have come?

This avenue boasts pizza places, a credit union, and farther on a Wal-Mart that did not exist when we lived here.

125

The Quick Cash Loans office turns my head. I used to park my car near the building's square profile five afternoons a week, back when it was a 7-Eleven.

Three years after marrying Tim and a while before motherhood, I worked the four to midnight shift by myself. Behind the counter and between shelves I assisted customers, sold Big Gulps, checked IDs of guys buying beer who looked early twenties like me. Across town Tim ran master control at the TV station until two in the morning.

Long-buried sensations sputter inside my chest. It's stupid, I decide, and yet driving through this end of town must be the culprit. Ancient emotions rise. I'm willing to give them a nod, but I plan to maintain composure.

Past the city limits our van follows curved lengths of highway nearing the campground. Ocean patches appear. Tim is silent now.

Managing a smile, I reach to pat his knee. "You doing okay?"

"I'm wondering why the oscillator on the digital modulator is still unstable and keeps causing the frequency to drift. I'll probably have to go in and work on it tomorrow after we get home."

"Oh. Sorry."

"But otherwise I'm fine."

That's my techno guy.

LONG AGO

He's been in my life, basically, forever. When we tell

friends our parents all knew each other before we were born, eyebrows raise. Arranged marriage?

Hardly. Growing up I thought of Tim as that older boy whose family came to our house in Tacoma, Washington, every few summers to visit. Our parents sat on kitchen chairs on the patio, sipping juice and discussing life in the ministry. Ignoring me, Tim took apart and swabbed with alcohol our crackling stereo speakers. He fixed Mom's cassette recorder and rewired our doorbell.

In 1977 I turned seventeen and suspected Tim considered me differently. *A long time ago in a galaxy far, far away* emblazoned movie screens that summer. Tim asked me to ride in his '66 Ford, a cool car my brothers dubbed the Millennium Falcon. I went along, because regarding relationships, I spoke to myself in terms Darth Vader might have used: "Your training is now complete." I assumed the co-pilot's seat and tucked one leg beneath the other.

Tim said, "You should fasten your seatbelt."

"I do when I'm driving," I said.

Tim drove without mentioning it again. He handed me a map detailing the Milton-Fife area. "I noticed a couple trailer parks around there," he said, pointing. "See which way we turn after the exit."

The two of us zipped north on I-5.

"It's thirty miles from your house to where I work now," Tim said. "So I'd like to live in my travel trailer someplace in between."

"Oh?" I glanced at him sideways.

Tim grinned. "Since your mom always needs someone

to pick you up after work."

Mom had asked him to fetch me a few times from my aunt's jewelry shop downtown, after he'd shown up on a Friday or Saturday evening before supper. I hadn't minded seeing his face at the end of several boring hours behind the cash register.

We exited the freeway and took a winding road that turned out to be wrong.

"So when you said go right you meant we should turn left?" Tim said.

"Hmm. Maybe that *was* it," I said, spreading and rotating the map again.

Tim's morning-blue eyes twinkled. He didn't seem to mind being lost with me.

Finally we arrived at the Firs Mobile Park of West Milton, and Tim met the park owner, a gray-haired gentleman.

"That the missus?" he asked Tim, pointing to where I waited in the car.

"Uh, no," Tim said.

"Girlfriend?"

"Well, no."

"Sister?"

"No. Sort of a cousin."

We laughed all the way back to my house. Tim had signed papers and would move his trailer to a space rimmed by ancient spruce. That autumn Tim would ask me out. We two children of preacher men would begin navigating our sexuality on a planet more crazed and shadowed than the past few generations had foreseen.

By the next time I hopped in the Falcon for a ride with Tim, a Triple-A sticker on his glove box proclaimed FAS-TEN SAFETY BELT.

I buckled.

I decided, soon after Tim asked me, that marriage was the best idea for both of us. With our fathers we stood at the front of the church, plenty more pastors looking on and nodding their blessings. I never imagined I would one day jump ship.

GLIMPSE

We pull into the campground, set up our tent, and fix supper. Then we drive to a sheltered, rock-strewn beach where sunset's blush adorns dark veils beyond the surf.

Tim and our son head over before nightfall toward looming cliffs to peer inside a cave. I can't decide which direction to stroll along the firm sand.

To my left teenagers cluster near a parked car. Two guys shout and, laughing, begin a light scuffle. I choose a meandering route to the right. My longing to kick off shoes conflicts with fear of losing them in twilight's dimness. I pause, awkward.

Scanning gentle waves that wash into the cove, I catch a glimpse of something. A small round shape bobs between crests—the ebony head of a sea lion.

Smoothly it disappears. I strain to find it, but shadows and faint glimmers trick my eyes. Did I really see it? Yes. The sea lion is there, closer to shore and unmistakable.

I imagine a female—she watches me and wonders what makes a land creature stand silent in descending gloom. Perhaps the sea lion is a mother who hunts salmon for her children. Or maybe my fanciful kinship is with a younger ocean adult, away from her mate, seeking bearings.

SHARK GILLS

On an October afternoon in 1982 I wheeled out the floor mop bucket at 7-Eleven, my smock-covered torso bent to the task. My wedding ring adorned the hand steadying the wringer.

Video game sentinels bleeped in their corner. The glass front door's automatic ding announced an entrant. I looked up to see a familiar customer towering, grinning. I blushed.

"Busy today, huh?"

"Well, no. Just mopping." *Brilliant*, I thought.

"I'll take my Camel straights, if you can spare the time." His hair, lighter than Tim's, brushed his blue jacket's collar.

As I hurried behind the counter for BJ's cigarettes more customers came in. BJ quipped, "Hey, Ditzy, you getting that divorce yet?"

"What? No."

He liked to tease, to catch me off-guard. Often BJ showed up several times during my shifts to buy odds and ends or play Ms. Pac-Man. "I'm a laid-off longshoreman," he'd confided once, leaning against the Slurpee machine while I restocked cups.

Counting his change, I attempted to return BJ's banter. I

fumbled and sensed my cheeks coloring more.

BJ shook his head, flashed his smile. "Later, Ditzy," he said.

In three years with Tim I hadn't let my attention stray to another man. Once a memory of an old boyfriend briefly invaded a dream, shaking me awake. I'd tucked it firmly inside a back closet of my mind.

Now I found myself watching for BJ's car to again halt in front of the dinging door, the vents on its front fenders like a shark's gills.

After work I waited at home for Tim, tunes pulsing through our dim rooms from my favorite Journey album, *Escape*. When he arrived, as had become Tim's habit, he went to his collection of radios—a CB base station and some others—through which he traded stories with truckers and old men on wireless sets 'til not long before dawn.

"I wish you were as eager to see me as those gadgets," I said from his workroom doorway.

Tim's eyes shone excitement. "I've found this neat bunch of people," he said. "They're on every night."

I yawned. "I bought a bag of candy at work for the trick-or-treaters."

"Not *this* soon," Tim said, smirking. "You'll eat every piece by tomorrow. We'll have nothing to give those poor little kids."

"I don't eat that much candy! Why do you talk like I'm out of control, or fat, or...?"

Tim grinned. "I don't think you're *too* fat."

I whirled away, stomping.

"You're just so much fun to tease."

Drifting off in our waterbed, I heard one scratching voice ask Tim, "You got a wife waitin' in the other room? *I wouldn't stay on air too long.*"

"Oh, she's sleeping," Tim replied.

Near Christmas they replaced the Donkey Kong video game at 7-Eleven with a new one called Dig Dug.

As I breezed between store shelves, the cooler stocked and my shift finally over, BJ slid quarters into the new machine. When I stepped out of the office with sweater and purse, he glanced up at me.

"Stupid game," he remarked.

"How do you play?" I asked.

"Come here and I'll show you."

BJ stood behind me. "Your turn first," he said. His fingers guided my hand. "There. Make the digger guy drop that rock on the monster." While I tried, BJ's thumb nudged my wedding band.

I focused halfway on the thrumming game. Just learning something new, I said to myself. No sense going home until Tim's done at the station.

Another regular, Cal, a wiry man who knew the store owner, came in around one. Cal got coffee and chatted with the burly young guy who worked graveyard. "Hey there, Dee," he said to me with a nod.

"I'd better head home," I said, watching BJ get close to Dig Dug's fifth level.

"Damn!" BJ exclaimed, swatting the joystick control. "Oh, sorry, Ditzy. Later."

By January I had to tell myself, driving west through town to the store, everything was under control. Anything's possible. But nothing's inevitable.

I tried to talk to Tim. At home on our waterbed watching *Dr. Who* I organized words and constructed vague questions.

"Would you dive into a pool you know might be empty?" I asked close to my husband's shoulder. Tim remained engrossed in the show.

"What do you think it's really like on the dark side?"

Tim glanced my way. "Huh?"

He just totally doesn't get me, I thought.

One February evening I paced behind the 7-Eleven counter. When BJ came in I slipped him a folded paper. On it were words, penned to suit, I hoped, a relationship blooming. They spoke my fantasy of strolls near the ocean, getting to know one another, the longings of love.

He read it. "What's this bullshit?" he said low.

I swallowed.

"You got a pen?" He scribbled something. "I can meet you at this motel." His smile spoke desire, and my own answered in kind.

Later I met him there. Just the one night. Afterward BJ drove away in his shark-faced car.

LOW TIDE

I wander the shore. My sea lion companion is gone.

Tim and our son stride up. "That's a pretty deep crevice

between the rocks," he says about the cave they ventured into. My husband's face seems to shine in the gloaming.

I throw my arms around Tim's chest and hold tight, promising both of them s'mores when we reach camp. My husband feels solid, alive, and his features appear calm. It's never been easy looking at him to discern pain's residue.

If men and women with a history somehow magically developed telepathic abilities, I would toss Tim a question: *Are you thinking about Memorial Day weekend, 1983?*

Next morning, an hour past sunrise, I scoot my chair close to Tim's steady campfire. Savoring a bowl of oatmeal, I sip hot cocoa and watch sun-swords cast themselves between fir boughs. Tim has taken our son to meet up with classmates and teacher on a beach exposed by an ultra low tide. I asked the guys if they minded my staying behind. Lazy, perhaps, but I've decided I'll accept these rare moments to linger and reflect.

MY CHOICE

After that winter night with BJ, I recognized two things. Because God doesn't miss a whisper I was done for, my marriage wrecked. Sooner or later the Creator would destroy me. Also, I disgusted myself. Though somehow certain that BJ would never return, I still wanted him.

I don't recall whether I imagined maintaining a sophisticated pose around Tim. But the next kiss from my husband, a day or two later, dislodged my secret.

"I've wronged you," I told Tim, chin to my collar. "In the

worst way." He shuddered as he sought composure. No tools at his workbench could mend this.

The next weeks we stayed together, stepping around each other. His days off Tim traveled two hours to the valley. Up and down I-5 he sought a job to ferry us inland. When he returned he spent whole nights organizing my haphazard linen closet and waxing the utility room floor.

At work I watched in vain outside the storefront for BJ's car. Tulips opened beside the credit union across the street. The sky darkened later each evening.

One busy night BJ pulled in. Behind the counter I held my breath while the customer ahead of him finished. Then I ventured a smile.

A woman with stringy hair stepped up as he asked for his Camels. "You forgot the milk," she said to him, holding forth a gallon.

"Damn it, woman," he replied. "Get in the car."

I took his money and turned away. As the door dinged I slammed the cash register closed.

Next morning I glanced sidelong at Tim as he buttered toast. Wishing to loosen the set of his jaw I asked softly, "How are you?"

Tim looked up. "How soon can you quit 7-Eleven?" His words were granite. "I heard back from Portland a week ago, and I'll start training at KPTV next Monday."

"But—so soon?"

"There's a hotel right across the street, until I can find us a place to rent."

"I'll have to give notice. They'll have to get someone else.

It might take a while." My heart thudded. I hadn't wanted to consider we'd really move away.

The first of May, Tim started running camera at KPTV. I stayed behind to pack and to finish at 7-Eleven.

A bizarre sensation enveloped me. I felt as though I viewed someone else, a woman on a movie screen, acting out these moments in my history. Evenings off the woman danced alone in my room to records, my soundtrack. I watched her obsess over a man who drove a shark car and smoked Camels.

"Hey, Dee, how you doing?" Cal, the wiry customer who was friends with my boss, waited across the counter at 7-Eleven to pay for coffee. "You need to talk to someone?"

"Oh, not really."

"I noticed you haven't played Dig Dug for a while."

"No."

"I'll be here when you get done tonight. Maybe help you fill the cooler."

"Thanks."

With Tim away, I began spending time most nights after work with Cal. We took walks through town in the tangy air. "Tell me something," he'd say. He asked questions about who I was. What I thought of life and death and religion.

"I'm sure God is mad at me," I told him one night. "I felt like this before I got married, when Tim and I nearly went all the way." I chuckled at the irony.

"But now," I said, "I just have to continue and stay married. To do what's right."

"If you think so," Cal said. "You seem real unhappy to me, though. Why don't we go for a drive?"

Stars blinked at us through amorphous clouds. The beach was sheltered.

"Dee," Cal said. "Come here. Let's quit fooling—I want you." A thrill pricked my scalp.

"Can we kiss and not tell?" I asked him.

But I told Tim. We met mid-month, midway between coastline and city. "I can't live with you in Portland," I said. "I've made my choice, and this is goodbye."

Back at our place I began separating my unruly stuff from Tim's. I set my wedding ring in a box in a drawer.

For a week or two I allowed the movie me to indulge in a montage, its soundtrack a carefree pop tune. With her new man, Cal, she picnicked, hiked, and went fishing by day. Late nights they hung out in various entertainment spots and at the homes of some of his friends.

The people she met related their stories of dealing with exes, of getting on with life's details. They drank, smoked, and laughed on cue.

I stayed mainly at Cal's, a tiny house with dilapidated vehicles in the yard. A vague plan emerged between us to move my boxes over from the place Tim and I were vacating.

My fix-it husband obtained a do-it-yourself divorce kit. He arranged to see me on the coast, bringing the papers the Saturday of Memorial Day weekend. By the time he showed up on our doorstep Tim was drunk.

"I wanted to tell you I've been praying," he said, missing the chair I offered and thudding on the floor.

Despite a heavy heart, I nearly laughed. I'd never seen him this way, definitely full of the spirit. I sat beside him.

Tim continued. "I said to God, why has this happened? And you know something?"

"What?"

"I realized I don't want to lose you. I want our marriage."

Tim told me he longed to rebuild our life, to start again.

"I ordered the divorce kit, but it's a last resort. I don't want a lawyer involved; they expect the process to divide us, so they can get paid. I want this to end in us finding a way back together."

I glanced past Tim. Through the workroom door his radios sat silent, unused for many weeks.

"I've been unfaithful to you," I said. I remembered the hardness in his voice the day he'd announced we were moving.

"But," Tim said, "I broke *my* vow to cherish *you*. I haven't cherished you the way I should've." He stood. "Excuse me."

Tim ran for the bathroom and remained there a long time.

I opened a window to the evening breeze. My brain felt linty. All I could think about was Tim saying, before we married, how glad he was I had never been sullied by wild living or another man.

It's way too late, I thought. I reached for a pen and signed the divorce papers.

Later as he stood pale before me I handed them to Tim. "I'm sorry," I said. "I don't know what I feel anymore."

"Could we at least try praying together?"

I stepped back. "What good would that do?" The words landed dully between us.

"Why not? We've tried everything else."

"But, *damn it*." I raised my purse and threw it on the table. Keys and Kleenex spilled. "I am *so* angry with God!" My outburst surprised us both.

We stood there.

"Okay," I finally said.

Knees on linoleum. Hands clasped. Tim's tears. Then mine. We prayed in clumsy voices.

Afterward we blew our noses. Somewhere in the neighborhood a child laughed, in the night where scents of barbecues lingered.

Tim drove to Portland. I made a phone call, then went to 7-Eleven. Cal stood talking, blowing on his coffee.

"Dee? What's going on?"

"I'm heading out of town, to stay with my parents," I said. "I just need to get far from this place so I can think."

"All right," he said. I slipped into my car while he walked to his. As I drove away I glimpsed him in the rearview mirror for the last time.

SHELTERED

Above our campsite a ceiling of heavy clouds builds. Soon, accompanied by chilled breezes, water drops. The tent is being pattered, and I move beneath its cover.

Memories could keep me absorbed for hours, but I figure the guys will head back in a bit. Besides, I would rather not dwell on the years when, during bad days with Tim, I grasped at shirttails, imagining one last rendezvous with Cal. I've learned the past never gets flushed away. Faded movie endings remain frozen behind the credits on screen.

COMING HOME

At my parents' home in June of 1983 I spent days on my childhood bed, reading, thinking, writing to Tim. "I don't expect anything from you," I wrote. "I'll take things slowly, maybe look for a job. See what comes next."

I imagined we might start over, meeting someplace, making tentative dates to wander flower gardens and museums. As it turned out, I got the flu.

My mom fixed chicken soup. Finally my temperature lowered. My hair a frizz mountain, I rose weakly onto an elbow when someone knocked at the bedroom door. "Come in," I said.

It was Tim. "I'd like to bring you home," he said. I knew then that I wanted to go with him.

In seasons to come I fretted and whined and rejoiced and laughed and gave birth and went to church with Tim beneath mundane skies.

Despite our best intentions, everydayness brought us more of ourselves. His wit sliced me; my emotions flummoxed him. And yet brighter realities showed up, too. Tim would take me in his arms when the kids left the house for an afternoon. I got us lost on back roads in the still-cool Millennium Falcon.

I puzzled over our story's implications. In the blessing of undeserved gifts I found a purpose and reason for wide-eyed, deliberate living. I couldn't have predicted the extent to which our grace would intrigue me, like a glimpse between breakers of someone standing in twilight on firm sand.

FAREWELL

At noon Tim and our son return and we navigate breaking soggy camp. Our boy says he barely noticed getting wet during his eventful morning around pungent tide pools brimming sea stars and anemones.

"Grab the other side of the tent," Tim tells him, tossing a rag. They stretch the fabric structure flat, wiping and folding.

Releasing tent pole sections, I sigh. "Being here sure brought back memories."

"Yeah," Tim says. "Terminal rain."

After he arranges everything to fit, we pile in the car. My turn to drive. I buckle up and stretch my arms. Tim reaches fast, tickles my ribs, then leans close for a moment.

I glimpse the squallish, empty ocean in the rearview mirror. East toward the valley, past damp fields and weathered barns lining the highway, I take us home.

Goodbye Upstairs

Mary Ellington

he Naval station where we lived when I was a child sat on the edge of Lake Michigan. Unlike Jacksonville where we moved after my father retired, a cold snap did not bring the city to a standstill. After fifty years I still remember one frosty morning in 1958 when my mother bundled me up, kissed my tiny bit of uncovered cheek, and pushed me out the door toward the bus stop.

Being dressed from head to toe in winter clothes made walking difficult. My coat, made of some kind of fake fur, proved to be more show than substance. My head sagged from the weight of a matching hat cinched under my chin with little fur balls hanging from the ties. Mittens kept my hands warm but rendered them useless. Heavy cotton tights covered my legs. Rubber galoshes fit over black and white oxfords. I waddled out the door like a well-wrapped mummy.

What might have been the perfect setting for a Currier

and Ives Christmas card looked more to me, at my tender age of seven, like pictures I'd seen of Russia where the Communists lived. This must be what my parents meant when they talked about the Cold War. To get to my bus stop I had to cross an icy street and climb a frozen hill. The same hill I could navigate with ease on a carefree summer afternoon posed a forbidding frozen challenge.

My first attempt at the hill was valiant but unsuccessful. I made it halfway up before beginning to slide back down. My rubberized feet had no traction. With nothing to grasp but ice I took an ungraceful tumble. I stood and ventured upward several more times. However, each endeavor met with the same result. I wasn't getting anywhere. With a flair for the dramatic, I lay on my snow-crusted stomach and attempted to swim up-hill like a love-sick salmon heading for the Promised Land.

Giving up, I lay on the frosty sidewalk waiting for whatever came first, summer or the Russians. Sunlight reflected off the ice. Tears froze to my face, blurring my vision even further. I sensed rather than saw a figure standing over me. My father reached down and helped me up.

<hr/>

Today my father is ninety-three years old. He has cancer. Most of his days are spent in quiet solitude, yet on occasion, Dad throws back his head and lets out a frustrated roar. The man who has always been in charge cannot control his own passing. Sitting at the kitchen table doing crossword puzzles, he withers at a slow pace.

Not long ago, in an unexpected burst of energy, Dad decided to sort through every closet in the house. Unsure if he was looking for something in particular or just wanted to clean house, I volunteered to help. I got to hold the flashlight.

Dad has lived in the same house since 1962. Over the years the room that sits atop the garage has become a repository of things my mother, if given the slightest opportunity, would have tossed in the garbage years ago. A self-proclaimed pack rat, my father held onto stuff even he can't remember. He rooted through musty cardboard boxes as if on a treasure hunt.

Dad's hands, covered with skin made fragile by blood thinners, lingered over every rediscovered prize. An intricately carved monkeypod statue from his time overseas. A pen set with interchangeable nibs given to him by former shipmates. Inflatable mattresses that no longer inflate. It was obvious to me that this stuff was useless, but my father handled everything from broken picture frames to rusted-out camping gear as if cradling a newborn baby. Dad took his time. I, on the other hand, grew restless. I had trouble understanding the significance of possessions that had been locked away and long forgotten. Why didn't he just throw it all in the trash and be done with it?

Watching Dad lost in memories, I was suddenly jogged from my self-indulgent indifference. This exercise had more to do with grieving than cleaning. Once I understood this was something Dad must complete at his own pace, I sank down in an old chair covered in fading chintz to wait. I didn't want to rush him. I did my best to give him a quiet, sacred space to savor his memories and make his farewells.

In the stillness of the room, I became aware of my father's labored breathing as he pulled a heavy coat from the cedar-lined chest he'd given my mother as an engagement present. Tarnished gold buttons that once passed military inspection and holes large enough to poke your fingers through were proof that there is no need for a wool overcoat in Florida.

After a while, the boxes were resealed and stuffed back in the closet. Dad appeared weary, anxious to return to the comfort of his chair. I've learned my father prefers to have no help at all rather than too much. Turning off the light, I stood behind him, aware that if he tripped all I could do was watch as he tumbled. I needn't have worried. Dad can still find a solution to most any problem. Undaunted by the flight of stairs before him, he dropped to his butt. Too weary to walk down ten steps, the man who once helped me scale a snowy hill ka-thumped his way down the stairs.

"Goodbye upstairs," Dad said, resting on the bottom step. There was finality in his voice, strong and frail at the same time. As he attempted to stand on tired legs, I reached down to help him up.

Dummy Dora

Eva M. Chapman

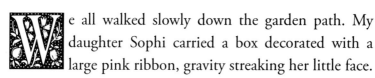e all walked slowly down the garden path. My daughter Sophi carried a box decorated with a large pink ribbon, gravity streaking her little face. A passerby might have thought that the box contained a beloved pet, perhaps a gerbil or a mouse. But no, what lay nestled in the box was her dummy.

Also called a pacifier or a soother, the dummy had been Sophi's constant companion for four years. Not the same one—that would have been far too unhygienic. There had been several over the years: pink, yellow, white; oblong, round, square; large, small, medium; all ending up in her mouth, covering her rosebud lips with what looked like a miniature plastic target. A target that may as well have been laid over my heart.

"Spoils her face," many said.

"She'll have buck teeth," said others.

"Gathers dangerous germs!"

"Sucking that monstrosity will keep her babyish."

And more seriously, often thought and not said:

"How ugly."

"Can't have been weaned properly."

"Looks like a neglected child."

"Poor mite. She has a bad mother."

All aimed at me. Arrows dipped in little indelible blobs of ink, staining my heart.

I was guilty as charged. But I plead mitigating circumstances: I was in my early twenties when I had Sophi. My own mother had been swallowed by schizophrenia in a mental hospital. My husband traveled overseas for study. I was left alone with a tiny baby, just four days old.

My friends didn't understand. They wouldn't have babies until their mid-thirties. The baby screamed all night. I breastfed incessantly. My nipples became cracked. In desperation I bought a dummy.

Peace.

Sophi loved the dummy. She loved it even better when I dipped it in honey. And I carried around a jar.

I joined my husband in France. I had to stop breastfeeding when Sophi was three months old, so I could teach. The dummy became a fixed feature. From time to time the dummy got lost. Disaster. I attached it to a piece of string which I tied around her neck. An imperious madame on a bus tut-tutted at me in French. Apparently I was endangering my child's life with possible strangulation. So I bought six dummies and placed them in various strategic places.

As disapproval, both external and internal, mounted, I tried to keep the dummy away from my child.

"I don't know where your dummy is," I told Sophi. But she had an uncanny sense of where a dummy was hidden. She spotted the small bulge in my cardigan pocket.

"There 'tis, Mummy."

"That's a tissue."

"No, there 'tis!"

Even when I carefully disguised the bulge in my pocket, she could hear the rubber nipple sliding against the plastic when I walked.

Sophi was an adorable little girl, witty, pretty, funny, articulate. She made the most delightful rabbit face with her lips when she wanted to kiss. But once she put that dummy in her mouth, she changed personality. She sucked away doggedly, drearily, never participating in conversations, never smiling. Just like a contented cow, chewing its cud. I called her Dummy Dora.

When she was four years old, it was time for her to begin preschool. The dummy had to go. Dummy Dora had to go too. I came up with the idea of the funeral.

As Sophi stood before the hole in the ground, she shook the box with the pink ribbon and heard the satisfying rattle of the dummy for the last time. She lowered the box and said, "Well, Dummy Dora, I have to go to school now. Goodbye!" We scooped the earth over the box and Sophi placed a flower on top.

Now Sophi has a little girl of her own, Elkie. Her older brother Cassidy never had a dummy. But Elkie does. She loves her dummy. Like her mother, she is bright, feisty, intelligent and vivacious. She even makes the same delightful rabbit puckering of her lips when she kisses. But when that dummy goes into her mouth, her vibrant personality changes. We call her Dummy Dora. She doesn't care.

I watch this development in my granddaughter's life with amazement. Sophi is a superb mother, and her husband Paul is a wonderful hands-on father. Elkie has everything a child should have and many things Sophi did not—thirteen months of breastfeeding, a happy stay-at-home mum, a devoted grandmother, lots of security and stability. But Elkie still loves and craves her dummy.

Observing my Dummy Dora grandchild is a healing experience for me. The dummy is no longer a source of shame. I no longer beat myself up with the "Bad Mother" stick. Dummy Dora and Elkie Lois happily coexist.

In my mind's eye, I return to that funeral over thirty years ago. My heart is lighter. I can now bury that box with the pink ribbon properly. I can finally say goodbye to my guilt and shame.

Lotus, Falling

Katrin Horowitz

We learned that my mother was dying when I spoke to her doctor late on the first Tuesday in May. My husband Andy and I had just arrived from Toronto, thinking we would stay with her for a week or so to help build up her strength for a heart operation that her cardiologist had been recommending for years. She had finally agreed to the surgery—reluctantly—because she was feeling so tired. He had assured her that, with the surgery, she'd be going strong for another fifteen years.

But she had also been having some serious pain in her abdomen and her lower back. A few days before our arrival, her family doctor had scheduled a CAT scan. When we arrived and found her curled up in pain, I immediately called him. He explained to me that her CAT scan had revealed gall bladder cancer that had spread to her liver and adrenal glands. He added that she might live as long as six months.

It was surprisingly easy to tell my mother she was dying. Because I had phoned from her bedside, she had heard my "Oh, no" when the doctor told me what was going on. She looked at me and said, "It's not good news, is it?" And I said no as the tears ran down my face. But she never shed a tear. Instead, she started comforting me. She was ready to die. She had lived a full life, she had been a widow for four years, her children and grandchildren were all doing well—and she wouldn't need to have the heart surgery that she had been dreading.

Within minutes, the obvious relief that she was feeling made all three of us feel happier. Her tiny, pain-racked body relaxed and her face lit up with a serene smile. We began listing all the benefits of her not lingering on. She would never have to go into a nursing home. This was the beginning of May and her favorite time of year—she would never have to cope with another icy winter. She and my father had always planned to spend New Year's Eve of the year 2000 together—now that would happen, although not the way they had planned.

We hugged a lot and promised each other we would enjoy the next few months together. We would drive through the local hills and forests watching spring turn into summer, we would drink tea on the back porch overlooking the Susquehanna River and watch the new ducklings grow, we would cook her favorite meals and drink wine and refresh a lifetime of happy memories. At dinner that evening we shared a bottle of her favorite red wine—although she only had one small glass and ate very little.

The next morning she could only manage one cup of tea instead of her usual two. After breakfast she and I got ready to go for a ride as we had done so many times in the past. We would head into northern Pennsylvania and turn onto any road that appeared to lead to picturesque farms and forests and hilltop views. We especially liked old dirt roads that looked like they weren't used very often. Within an hour we would find ourselves thoroughly lost and delightedly exploring yet another byway or backwater. Then we would spend the final hour of our drive looking for clues that would take us back home, all the while laughing and talking about politics, religion and other foibles, books we had enjoyed, the latest in family gossip, jokes and memories.

But today was different. As I helped her into the car the sunshine highlighted how the jaundice had already colored her skin. And we had only driven for fifteen minutes when it was clear that she was enduring the ride, not enjoying it. She could only manage the nausea by an act of will that prevented her from talking. We headed home, with me in tears again because we had just lost something that had given us both such pleasure over the years. For different reasons, neither of us spoke on the return trip, but we held hands to comfort each other.

The losses had started years earlier. My father's decline into Alzheimer's before his death was long and sad. My mother first began to seem old and fragile during that time. Andy and I visited often, and our trips through the countryside had started as a way to give her a break from her constant caregiver role. Andy stayed behind to keep my father safe. The end of our rides together marked the beginning of a whole series of "last times" that led much too quickly to her death.

Later that week we visited her doctor, armed with a series of questions. She needed to know what was going to happen to her and how long it would take. But the doctor, a gruff, old-fashioned GP who expected us to defer to his expertise, evaded our questions with statements like, "You might still be with us in six months," and "You can go out and play football in the meantime." The discussion she had hoped to have, about pain management options and how she could keep her wits about her as long as possible, was stymied. When I pressed on despite his obvious impatience, he finally said, "How many more questions do you have? I have a waiting room full of patients." My mother's last visit to her doctor of twenty-seven years lasted less than fifteen minutes.

Her cardiologist, whom she happened to see in the waiting room, was even less helpful. He said, "Once we get the little problem with your liver taken care of, we can see about that surgery." The only useful development that came out of that exhausting and frustrating appointment was the decision to turn her care over to hospice. The hospice's role involved no active treatment, only the practical care that would keep her as comfortable as possible in her own home until she died.

The senior hospice nurse who came to the house the next day was more helpful, more empathetic, and much clearer about the timeframe: we were looking at possibly two or three months, probably less. But the questions my mother most wanted answered—what she could expect, and how messy it would get—the nurse sidestepped. On the positive side, the case nurse would visit at least once a week and there was round the clock telephone support if we had any problems. They would also provide equipment and other help so that she could stay in her home.

Meanwhile the losses continued. Reading was a pleasure that my mother and I had shared ever since I could remember. When I was little, the best day of the week was Friday, when she would go to the library during her lunch hour and choose a stack of books for me. When I was in my teens, we would both read a book and then talk about the decisions the heroine—all the books we really enjoyed had strong female characters—had made, and whether we would have done the same. We created a whole philosophy in exploring the moral and practical implications of choices that characters like Jane Eyre, Scarlett O'Hara, Becky Sharp and Madame Bovary made.

In more recent years, each of us happily passed on books, and I had brought with me several that I was sure she would like. But I discovered that reading now increased her discomfort, despite the addition of anti-nausea medication, and that it exhausted her to focus on a story. I never gave her those last books.

The first few days I was always on the edge of tears. I cried whenever I remembered yet another favorite activity that I could no longer share with her. But both Andy and I did our best not to let the tears leak out while we were with my mother. We felt we owed it to her to match her cheerfulness—to remember that our job was to make this time as happy for her as we could. We knew that our tears would only distress her.

Nevertheless, that first week of her dying was also a time that we enjoyed tremendously. She could still get out of bed for part of the day and even joined us at the dinner table, although she ate very little and never had wine again after that first evening. One warm day we were able to have tea on the back porch where she had always planted red and pink geraniums in the flower boxes. This year, I had planted them for her, and it felt so normal and right for her to be sitting in her favorite place in the whole world.

But she was most comfortable lying in bed on her right side, so I often stretched out next to her and we would talk together like a couple of teenagers. We were once again exploring those philosophical questions about how best to live—and die. We agreed that one of the benefits of the way she was leaving was that she would have a chance to say goodbye to everyone who mattered to her.

She would husband her strength until she could sound cheerful and energetic, like her old self, and then she would call—the European relatives and friends from her childhood, local friends, friends who had moved away. Everyone was comforted and strengthened by her attitude, even as they were shocked by her news. And after a call or two, she would take another pain pill and sleep almost comfortably.

Her strength diminished rapidly with each passing day. By the end of the first week, her double bed was replaced with a hospital bed, so she could sit up with less effort. She still insisted on getting up and dressed every day, because she said it made her feel better—and made her look forward to getting back into bed. And she still had the ability to laugh at the whole awkward process of dying. One day, as she was painstakingly walking from her bedroom to the kitchen, clutching at each piece of furniture in turn, she confided to me that she thought of her furniture as her support group.

She still joined us at the dining room table for dinner and we would try to tempt her with favorite foods. One morning she announced that she had dreamed about German hot dogs—something that had long been banished from her low-fat, heart-healthy diet. We served German hot dogs for dinner that evening and delighted in her enjoyment of two or three small bites.

The pain was visibly increasing, but she took little pain medicine, because she wanted her mind to be clear. One cool, sunny afternoon during our second week with her, we moved her onto a chaise in the garden so she could enjoy her azaleas in full bloom. That was the afternoon my brother and his family arrived from Wisconsin. She alternately dozed and talked with us, rallying her strength and smiling, especially when the children were around. That evening I made one of her favorite dishes, chicken paprikash, on what turned out to be the last time we sat at the dining room table together.

By the beginning of the third week, both my brothers had visited, she had listened to a final concert from two grandchildren, and watched a couple of baseball games with her youngest grandson. It was especially important to her that her grandchildren should have happy memories of the last time they were with her.

One of the final milestones came a few days later, when my daughter, her oldest grandchild and an accomplished photographer, arrived from California. She brought with her a photograph she had taken a year earlier: my mother looking at the camera—the photographer, rather—with her loving smile and twinkling eyes, a wine glass in her hand, and the fresh new leaves of a tree shimmering in the background. My mother showed it proudly to every friend who came to visit.

One afternoon when she was heading back to bed for a rest, she collapsed to the floor, much to my daughter's dismay, and then insisted on crawling the rest of the way. But when she told me what had happened, she said it was really quite graceful—that she had felt like "a lotus blossom drifting gently to the ground." We enjoyed the image, but also made sure we had a wheelchair on hand whenever she got out of bed.

The next day, my daughter's fiancé arrived. We had a wonderful afternoon on the porch, where we talked and laughed and took photographs that show how relaxed and happy my mother was that day. She gave each of us gifts to remember her by—family heirlooms that she wanted to give "with warm hands" as her mother had given them to her. We talked about the kind of funeral she wanted to have. And that she would like me to plant a lilac bush with deep purple blossoms for her, a companion to my father's memorial tree that had been growing in my front yard for the past four years.

But she was eating little more than a few spoonfuls of

soup or yogurt, and she needed more and more back rubs to keep the pain at bay. Rubbing her back became a shared pleasure, because we could feel her relax under our fingertips, and she would always whisper, "I love you" before she drifted off to sleep.

At the start of the fourth week, just after my daughter left, the hospice nurse visited again. When we had first met this short, wide woman in late middle age with eyes that headed off in two directions, we all had doubts. But she brought both wisdom and practical experience to her work. My mother and I even let her call us "Dear" and "Sweetie." Ordinarily, we would have rejected those meaningless, often demeaning terms—my mother graciously, me more forcefully—but somehow it fit the occasion, and she clearly liked both of us.

On this visit, she spoke about how my mother had now finished her life's work and that it was time to deal with the increasing pain with stronger medication. My mother agreed that it was time for morphine. The nurse told Andy and me that our job was to prevent her from feeling pain, and that we should use the morphine as much and as often as necessary.

This marked the start of the final phase of her dying. For several days my mother faded in and out of sleep, passively content when she was awake and sleeping more comfortably and more often. She left her bed only to go to the bathroom, and even that was an exhausting undertaking. Characteristically, she worried about being too much trouble for us, but she always smiled when we told her that it was a privilege to be with her. During that increasingly difficult time, what made both of us happiest was simply to hug and kiss. When she was ready to sleep again, I often cuddled up next to her and took her in my arms. She said, "This feels so good. I love you." And then she slept peacefully.

Just a few days later, even though she was barely conscious and very confused from the massive amounts of morphine, she hugged me tightly and said, for the last time, "I love you, Katrin." Her love was the last thing that remained after a month of losses. It was more than enough.

She died in her sleep early in the morning of the second of June. After her ashes were buried next to her husband, her family and closest friends gathered on her back porch to celebrate her life with food and wine and flowers, laughter and tears. She had specified no tears, but we couldn't help it. Most importantly, we told each other many wonderful stories about her life and how she had made all of our lives better. It was the funeral she had wanted.

Turning in My Keys

Ann Ingalls

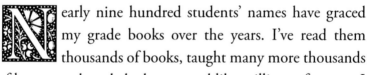 early nine hundred students' names have graced my grade books over the years. I've read them thousands of books, taught many more thousands of lessons and graded what seemed like millions of papers. I looked forward to each and every day. No two were alike and each day I knew I made a difference.

Thirty-seven years is a long time to do anything, especially when you try to do it to the best of your ability. My time to leave had come. Younger, fresher voices needed to be given a chance to try out new techniques.

Still, it was hard to leave the classroom where children and I laughed, danced, held spelling bees and math mad minutes, played round robin, painted, learned to stack blocks, practiced writing in manuscript or cursive, and took care of pets and each other. I had even done cartwheels for the children when projects had been successfully completed.

My students have become parents, educators, service workers, engineers, and doctors. They are dancers, artists, chefs, police officers, nurses, computer geniuses, and construction workers. They are builders and bakers and childcare workers and environmental specialists. I have a couple of pharmacists and dentists, firefighters and stay-at-home moms. When I see them now, they give me big bear hugs and ask, "Can you still wiggle your ears?" I can and so I do.

And I'm proud of each and every one of my students. Spending time with them was my chosen career and my privilege. I never made a bundle of money but I've had the pleasure of helping children learn to read, write, solve math and science problems, and learn about the larger world.

Will I miss it? Sure. I'll miss the smiles, hugs, tying shoes for little feet, passing the tissue box and offering encouragement to a child who is struggling, then seeing that same child succeed. All of it is just plain hard work, but it's worth the effort to hear a child say, "Look what I can do," and know I had a small part in that, if only in teaching him how to pump his legs on a swing.

When the last month arrived, I averaged grades, took children to the lunchroom and recess for the last few times, played chess or quiet ball with kids during indoor recess, took them to assemblies and passed on whatever information I thought would be useful. Don't forget to tie your shoes. Have you got your lunch card? Did you remember to do your homework? How can I help you?

After all, teaching is like parenting, only to a group of twenty-six or more at one time. I was stretched as far as possible, and yet, in the end, I grieved terribly about leaving my much-loved charges. I knew the teacher who would replace me. She is talented and caring, hard-working and effective. The children would be in good hands.

So, on the very last day, when all the students had departed and I cried my eyes out, when all the shelves had been cleared and teaching supplies had been stored, when my classroom inventory was complete and filed in the office, when final grades were reported and I signed off on each permanent record, I touched my desk, listened one more time to the voices that echoed through this sacred space, and silently closed the door.

I allowed myself one last look at the old brick building. Lots more learning will go on there. From now on, I'll be learning about the larger world outside the classroom and meeting up with a few old friends.

I hugged my principal and our school secretary, tossed my keys on the counter, turned and walked away.

Saying Goodbye to a Faithful Companion

Robert B. Robeson

Everyone has a hard-luck story. Take mine. After nearly a decade of the closest possible physical relationship—this side of marriage—I recently lost a warm and faithful companion in a moment of blind and savage passion.

I'm not into tweed jackets, ascot ties, $600 Gucci loafers, or lying on a beach sipping piña coladas. What I do is spend large blocks of time writing in my office while wearing my favorite brown jogging suit. Making myself comfortable shouldn't be a big deal. Everyone knows it's unrealistic, illogical, and irrational to expect a successful writing performance (or any other kind of performance) if you're uncomfortable. Herein lies the rub.

About ten years ago, my wife (who's always been the type of person who believes that going shopping will save

165

us money) helped me select a jogging suit for exercising. It was light brown with a dark brown stripe down the outside seam of both legs. A strip of elastic encircled the waist and fit my moderately sleek physique. It accompanied me around the neighborhood on evening jaunts, helped me to relax on weekends, and kept me warm during those cold Nebraska winters in my secluded and austere office.

Through succeeding years, its elastic waistband expanded with my girth and did its best to keep various parts of my anatomy from being exposed to the elements or annoying criticism from total strangers. It was as if that jogging suit wasn't a wad of cloth, after all. It was my buddy. It had grown out of shape with me.

Like death, taxes, and *The Honeymooners* reruns, I thought this jogging suit would last forever.

Each evening and weekend I'd slip into my brown writing uniform, like King Arthur's knights used to put on their armor in Camelot, and go to work. Every time a full moon made an appearance, I'd throw it in the washing machine whether it needed it or not. I kept thinking that this process was shrinking the pants, but my wife said "the plant had merely outgrown the pot."

Okay, so the suit *was* older than vermin and I didn't have that high-gloss, show-biz shimmer and shake like before, but that didn't give her the right to insult the two of us. I mean, I *reeeeeeeally* loved that jogging suit. When I had it on, I could write so fast I'd create downdrafts with all of the paper flying around my desk.

One evening I went to my closet to change before my writing session began.

"Have you seen my brown jogging suit?" I asked my wife.

"Old jogging suits never die, they just fade away," she said.

"I didn't know you were a fan of General Douglas MacArthur. Where is it?"

"That number's been retired," she replied. "It looked and smelled like a well-trampled game preserve after the rainy season. I even had to tip our curbside sanitary engineer before he'd take it to its final resting place."

"You threw out my favorite writing outfit…without even asking me?" I whined, slumping into the nearest chair. Now I knew how Linus felt when Snoopy snatched his blanket.

The real question here is whether a wife has the right to arbitrarily trash any of her husband's valued and sentimental objects without permission. Newspaper clippings substantiate the fact that lots of guys have walked in front of trains, cars, and buses on purpose. Perhaps they had a wife like mine.

I intend to keep my options open on whether retribution is a proper course of action to take. See, she has this favorite negligee that was purchased sometime around the Boer War. It scratches me like crazy. It's like sleeping beside a rose bush. Maybe, with a little financial remuneration, our curbside sanitary engineer could do me a favor, too.

Puppy Love

Susan Weich

ix months after my yellow Lab Bailey died of kidney failure, I was ready for a new best friend.

I was committed to getting a dog from a shelter, and a puppy's picture on one of the websites in early February caught my eye. Her name was Valentine, and she was a ten-week-old mutt.

"She's a rescue from a wonderful, caring person who took in her pregnant mom," the listing said.

I called the number and spoke to the puppy's foster mother.

"I almost didn't put this dog up for adoption because I love her so much," the woman said. "She's drop-dead gorgeous and incredibly smart."

My son and I drove an hour to a ranch on the southwestern edge of the metro area to see Valentine. She was a fluff ball with legs and a tail. A black streak of fur ran down

169

her back, and she had different colored eyes—one blue, one brown.

Valentine's foster mom left us alone with the dog to get acquainted, and I asked my son for his first impression.

"She's the one," he said.

By that time the puppy had climbed into my lap, and I was stroking her super-soft fur. It was a love connection for both of us.

My son and I decided right away that we wanted to give the puppy a new name. We tried out all kinds of crazy ones on the way home—names of streets we passed and gas stations and shopping centers. We settled on Sydney because her foster mom thought she might be part Australian shepherd.

That weekend was the happiest I'd been since Bailey died. There's just something about a dog in the house that makes it feel more like a home.

We took her shopping and filled her cart with crunchy treats and a red and white rope pull. We played with her in the yard and showed her off to the neighbors.

Potty training was a bit more challenging. The third night we had her, Sydney had an accident in the computer room. While I was cleaning that up, she started throwing up on the expensive rug under our dining room table. I flushed the mess down the toilet, and then the toilet backed up.

As I was using a plunger on the toilet, I heard Sydney throwing up again. I picked her up and held her as I surfed the Internet for tips on dog training. What I didn't know was that Sydney was showing the first symptoms of parvovirus. When her stomach troubles continued the next day, I took her to our veterinarian.

Sydney had been vaccinated against parvo, but she hadn't gotten the whole series of puppy shots yet because she wasn't old enough. That made her susceptible to the serious disease, which the vet said was similar to the flu. She advised me to take Sydney to an animal hospital where she could get twenty-four-hour care. Dogs that got intense medical treatment had an 80 percent chance of recovery, she said. I had caught it early, and she was a sturdy eleven-pound pup, so her chances were good.

I rushed her to the hospital. Because parvo is so contagious, Sydney had to be put in an isolation ward. A technician dressed in a green hospital gown, mask and gloves carted her away. Sydney was a very social dog, so she didn't like being by herself. As the vet explained her treatment, we could hear the dog yapping in the next room.

"That's a good sign—she's strong," the vet told me.

The next three days I visited and called several times to get updates on her condition. They wouldn't let me touch her, so the best I could do was talk to her and blow kisses from the hallway. The prognosis was cautiously optimistic.

Early Sunday, the vet wanted to give Sydney some plasma, and I gave the okay. When I went to see her later, I told one of the vet assistants that I was worried, and she told me not to give up hope.

When I called around 9:00 p.m., another assistant said Sydney was sitting up in her cage and seemed to be improving, so I was totally unprepared for the 5:15 a.m. call the next morning.

"We're performing CPR on Sydney," the voice said. "Do you want us to continue?"

It took me a moment to comprehend the question.

"I'm sorry, but I'm going to need an answer. Should we continue CPR?"

How could this be happening to the same puppy that was chasing me around the yard a few days ago? We barely knew each other and now I had to decide whether to end our relationship.

Finally, I told them to stop treatment. I didn't want her to suffer. The vet told me she had fought hard, but she was gone.

I got dressed and grabbed a rose from the flower arrangement my husband had given me for Valentine's Day.

When I got to the animal hospital, a tech asked me to sign pages of paperwork and pay the balance of the $2,000 bill, and then handed me a clear plastic bag that held Sydney's collar. It was pink leather and adorned with the initial "S" in rhinestones.

I was numb as the woman led me to the back room. Before she closed the door, she said to take as much time as I needed.

The room was decorated just like the treatment room I had been in a few days earlier when everyone was more optimistic. It had the same antiseptic smell, the same black plastic chairs, the same wallpaper with its pouncing puppies and curious kittens.

Sydney was lying on her side on a stainless steel table. Her fur was matted and wet, and she was cold because the techs had mistakenly thought I wouldn't be coming, so they had put her in the freezer. Her right leg was shaved, and the remains of an IV were taped to it.

I thought about how different this was than my last moments with Bailey. She was twelve and suffering when I made the decision to put her down. I remember watching the vet push the pink-colored drug down the plunger and seeing it go in through the IV. As I held Bailey, she drifted off after a little cough. She was my first dog, and she had been a gentle, loyal friend. I had lots of happy memories of her, and I clung to them long after she was gone.

I didn't get the chance to have many good times with Sydney. The memory I decided to keep was the one on the car ride back from my daughter's hockey game the night before she got sick. Sydney rested her head on my forearm and fell asleep in my lap. That had convinced me that she and Bailey were kindred spirits.

As I looked at her battered body now, all I could see was the beautiful puppy that had stolen my heart ten days before. I stroked her and kissed her muzzle. I placed the rose under her paw and told her that Bailey would take care of her until I saw her again.

The Guest in My Mother's Home

Maryann McCullough

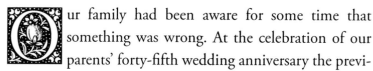 ur family had been aware for some time that something was wrong. At the celebration of our parents' forty-fifth wedding anniversary the previous month, my mother's left arm had been in a blue canvas sling because it was more comfortable, not as heavy. And shopping, which she had always pursued with marathon-like endurance, no longer occupied her days. Because my mother was diabetic, neuropathy was the original diagnosis—but not the final one.

On August 10, a call came from my brother Jay. Amyotrophic Lateral Sclerosis. The words were unfamiliar, but when he explained, "She has Lou Gehrig's disease," I understood. I knew it would make a difference in the way my mother lived. But I couldn't know how much it would change our lives.

My first thoughts were of the inappropriateness of the

diagnosis. My mother had never been a respecter of illness. Staying home from school to go shopping with her was reasonable, but colds or cramps were nothing. "You'll be fine," she'd say. "Offer it up."

Our father, on the other hand, was comfortable with a multicolored assortment of pills. Most of his children attribute his longevity to our mother's lack of coddling. For her, life was too full to waste time being ill. We used to kid that our dad would get excited (even buying new pajamas!) when he had to go into the hospital. There he would receive sympathy and attention from the female staff. They recognized him as a gentle soul, appreciative of their tender loving care.

My father died of a heart attack, just weeks after my mother's ALS diagnosis, and thirty-three years after doctors had warned him to put his things in order because his days were numbered. They had been a good team, formed by an era where fathers did their part by providing well for their families while mothers "manned" the home front. Both of my parents were very good at fulfilling their respective roles. She loved the spotlight. He was the quiet listener. Her song of him was Bette Midler's "Wind Beneath My Wings." It was a fitting choice. But now she would have to make her way without that support.

I think of her strengths and wonder. If she had lived in a later generation would she—would they—have made the same choices? In so many ways, she was a woman born ahead of her time. It could have been she, rather than my dad, who was driven to work in a chauffeured limousine. She ran a house—complete with ten children—with the intensity of a Marine drill sergeant (a nice Marine drill sergeant) and with the effectiveness of a top CEO.

Saturday afternoons at 705 Franklin are among my favorite memories of her management style. There was an assembly line for children that included nail clipping, ear cleaning, shoe polishing, bang trimming, and crew cutting. Even stray neighborhood children got the full deal if they happened to be in the kitchen during the pre-Sunday cleanup.

My role as the firstborn was to be the responsible one. In my family I was more the assistant mother than one of the children. With a new baby coming every year or so, someone always needed to be fed or changed or bathed. If I wasn't always thrilled to do it, I did it nonetheless. Daughters are supposed to help their mothers. And I certainly thought of myself as a good daughter. Until the time of my mother's illness, that was how I saw myself. But by 1986 I was wearing the hats of wife, mother of three sons, and math teacher to many. And I was living nearly two thousand miles away in Phoenix, Arizona.

Back in River Forest, those little kids I'd helped mother had grown up. Most had acquired spouses. Some had produced a child or two. Many of them had settled in the suburb of their childhood, within walking distance of our parents' condominium. And they, unlike me, were the good daughters and sons who were still there.

My mother was as efficient with her illness as she was with the rest of her life. Within a scant three months of her diagnosis, she died. An illness that can linger for decades, slowly denying a person the control of his body, moved through my mother like a man on a mission.

By the mid-eighties, our big house had been replaced with a condominium. While lovely, by comparison it had a feeling of a miniature world. Off my parents' bedroom was a small television room. As the illness spread quickly through my mother's body, that little room became her world. A lounge chair served as her bed, throne, mission control, or spa chair as the needs of the day dictated.

The room was about ten feet square, and when I visited, it was usually standing room only. My mother was surrounded by tender loving care. This wonderful family she and my dad had created cooked for her. They fed her. They rubbed her legs. They even did those things that no one enjoys doing. They visited, but they also worked very hard.

I had been anxious for Labor Day weekend to arrive so I could go and care for her myself. But my visit and my role were not what I had expected. And though I would visit several times in the next few months, the pattern never varied.

My visits were occasions for my mother to have her lipstick applied by one of my sisters. She would greet me from her chair, dressed in some caftan-like creation, her hair pouffed from its bed-flattened position. If she had to use a bedpan, she asked me to call one of my sisters, and then requested that I leave the room. I was hurt. It didn't make sense. I had come all this way to assist her but I felt peripheral to the process of her care. I had just assumed that I would take over, be the responsible one. But that wasn't to be my role.

It was my sister Kitti whose insight turned the hurt into understanding. Just as decades earlier she put on gloves and fabulous big hats, my mother was getting dressed up for me. My visits from Arizona provided her a temporary respite from the dependence and indignity imposed by her disease—the opportunity for a few moments of a remembered life. It was not possible for her to live that life with her children who saw her day in and day out. But for a special short-term visitor she could reassume a life with decorum.

Within families, roles happen. She's the smart one. He's the comedian. My comfortable role, the responsible daughter, had been reassigned. I was now an extra in the cast of characters who were an integral part of my mother's last days. I recognized that the burden for those who cared for her daily needs was much greater than mine—both physically and emotionally. And her burden was the greatest of all. But I felt like an outsider, a guest within the walls of my mother's home. It was not the role of my choosing.

The last time I visited her, my mom was closer to her death than I realized. Her ability to speak was compromised, but we spent our time working a crossword puzzle together. Though her body was no longer under her control, she continued to challenge her mind. One point of pride was doing her crosswords in ink. And so, ballpoint in hand, I read the clue. Then placing my ear close to her lips, I listened carefully for her response and entered the letters in the little boxes.

This was how our time together ended. No drama. Just a quiet little crossword puzzle for two women who had loved each other for a very, very long time. We had each gone through a reassignment of roles. She had relinquished the helm of her life—and the helms of all those other lives she was so fond of directing. I, too, could let go of my previous role, and with new insight, understand and appreciate the value of my bit part in our family drama.

The Pink Thing

Ann Reisfeld Boutté

y mother, having been diagnosed with inoperable lung cancer, was in the hospital for the last time. Sitting in bed, still alert and relatively comfortable, she told me, "Pie, don't forget. My wedding ring is in the pink thing." Pie, short for Annie Pie, had been her nickname for me as long as I can remember. "I won't forget," I promised her.

I didn't know what the pink thing was, but I didn't want to worry her or tire her by asking unnecessary questions. I was confident that I would find it among her possessions without much difficulty.

Hours later, she suffered a setback that left her in pain and unable to speak. After her death two days later, the nurses gave me a plastic bag containing her belongings. In it were her eyeglasses, clothes, slippers, and a cosmetics bag. I took them home and placed them in a drawer in the spare room, unable at the time to deal with their disposal.

The ring she spoke about wasn't her original one. On my parents' wedding day—April 16, 1942—my father had given her a platinum band with diamond chips, a complement to her square-cut diamond engagement ring.

They had met ten months earlier at the wedding of mutual friends and had a short courtship before becoming engaged. They were married forty-nine years at the time of my father's death.

Sometime during those years, my mother decided that a plain band is often more practical and easier to clean, especially when cooking, one of her favorite pastimes. So on one anniversary, my father gifted her with a gold band that she interchanged with the platinum duo, depending on the occasion. She had given me the diamond rings some time earlier.

It took me several months to close her apartment. As I did, I combed every corner and examined every item in search of the ring. I was particularly careful to inspect everything in any shade of pink, from the softest shell to the deepest rose. But no matter where I looked, it eluded me.

I was afraid that the ring had been lost or stolen or, worst of all, thrown away. After months of fruitless searching, I resigned myself to the fact that it was gone. The notion that I could have inadvertently or carelessly discarded an object of so much sentimental value filled me with remorse.

Almost three years after my mother's death, my husband and I decided to tackle some much-needed redecoration in our home—new paint, wallpaper, and carpet. Before we began, we had to cull our belongings.

When I opened a drawer in our guest room, I found the forgotten plastic bag that I had brought home from the hospital. Even though pangs of loss still pained me, I felt it was time to let go and dispose of my mother's things.

I kept the eyeglasses. But I took one last look at the clothes, slippers and cosmetics bag, then dropped them in a trash bin and walked away. Ten steps later something drew me back. I turned around and retrieved the bag. Inside I found L'Oreal face powder, Botanical hand lotion, Chap-Stick and a crumpled tissue. When I unfolded the tissue, I found the gold band.

Then it dawned on me. Seen through weakened eyes, the delicate red and white design on the cosmetics bag blended into pink. The pink thing!

I considered sizing the band to fit me, but I decided against it. I have my own gold band. More importantly, sizing the ring would distort the inscription that reads, "Same Husband, New Ring." There's nothing about that I want to change.

A Bloody Good Party

Alison Cameron

So, Dad, have you thought about The Funeral at all?"

My sister Claudia rolled her eyes and went to make lunch.

I had no compunction asking such a delicate question. Dad was soon to get the results of a scan to see if his cancer had spread. He'd already told us, "I'm not expecting anything good." I wanted to bring up the topic of his funeral while it seemed far-off and unreal.

Besides, we had an understanding. I could ask whatever I liked. If he didn't want to answer, he'd stare off into the distance, pretend he hadn't heard, or grunt "Mmmm."

"Not so much the funeral," he said now, "but the reception after. Obviously we can't have it here." He gestured at his cozy living room, which we mentally populated with everyone he knew. No, they'd never fit.

"Maybe outdoors?" I suggested. My father's apartment building was constructed on the footprint of an old manor house, ten apartments on four acres of grounds. Imagine *Masterpiece Theatre*: mature trees and rhododendrons encircling sweeping lawns, fields of buttercups, horses across the narrow road.

"What if it rains?" he asked.

We contemplated rain, always a possibility in England, no matter the month.

"I know!" he said. "We could have a marquee on the lawn!"

For a moment we could pretend we were planning a summer fete, entranced by this vision of a large tent erected on the lawn of Hawley Lodge. But, "Where would they park?" Dad asked, and pffft! the vision dissolved. There was no parking. Two hundred people had come to my mother's funeral.

"Lots of them have popped off by now," said Dad, but even if only half came, it would be too many.

We regretfully abandoned the marquee, but Dad was still interested in the planning, so after lunch we drove to the crematorium where Mum's ashes were scattered to see what they could suggest.

Southern England looked stunning that day, as it did every day of Dad's illness: golden light, clear air, huge skies filled with billowy white clouds. We drove down leafy lanes, past picture postcard scenery—quaint villages, thatched cottages, fields of baby lambs.

We reached the crematorium, found a chap who worked

there and asked him a few questions, chief among them, "Where do people go afterwards for a reception?" He rattled off a pub, two hotels and a golf course clubhouse. The golf course was nearest so we started there.

It was surreal, people trundling about with golf carts and clubs, and us on our darker mission. When we entered the clubhouse, a pleasant young man stepped forward. "May I help you?" he asked.

We said we wanted some information about a reception after a funeral.

"Oh!" he said. "Do you have a date?"

"No. Not yet."

"Oh. You don't have a date then?"

How to explain? Finally Dad, a walking cadaver in his too-big sports coat, piped up. "I'm still living, aren't I?"

We laughed with relief. The young man's eyes widened. He understood—and rallied. "Ah! Doing a bit of pre-planning, are we?"

He showed us a room away from the golfers, with a separate entrance. He showed us various menus, explained about drinks. When we tried to estimate how many people would attend, he looked Dad in the eye and asked, "Just how popular are you, sir?" Claude and I said, "Very," while Dad looked modest.

The young man had sold us on his golf clubhouse. We made our goodbyes. Dad said, "Sounds like a bloody good party. I'm only sorry I shan't be here to enjoy it."

The young man gently took Dad's bony hand. "I don't quite know what to say to you, sir."

Dad said, "How about, 'See you later.'" Three of us blinked back tears.

When the time came to put the plan into action five months later, the clubhouse was already booked. But our helpful young man recommended another place, a stately home turned convention center, which was even better.

Because of Dad's "pre-planning," we knew he wanted to stand everybody one last drink. We knew what food he wanted us to order. When one hundred people showed up, and Dad's old Navy friend called out a toast in his big voice, "To Alan!" and everyone roared back, "To Alan!" I felt like cheering. It was perfect.

Somebody said, "It sounds strange to say, but I've had a wonderful time!" And that was the general feeling.

Dad got his "bloody good party."

The Mumo Letters

Dara Hodge-LaRue

Mumo,

Today was the first time since your funeral I was in Good
Shepherd Church—to celebrate the Resurrection of Christ,
of all things. You've been gone for twenty-seven days now,
and nothing is even close to normal. Easter has always been
a big deal to us, Gram, but no one is ready to face a major
holiday without you yet.

Mom tried her best to make it like you used to, but she
scorched dinner so badly that she abandoned her efforts and
handed the reins to Dad. Chris was strong for Mel and me,
as a big brother should be, because we just kept crying. He
kept Tont busy with a book of political cartoons that Mom
and Dad had put in his Easter basket so that Tont wouldn't
have to see us that way.

Tont keeps blaming himself. He says that if he had made sure the nurses at the hospital were turning you on your side like they were supposed to, then you would never have gotten a bed sore that big. The doctors tell us now that all the nurses had to do was move you every now and then. That makes me mad, Gram. You might still be here if it weren't for that.

Tonto said the Mother Mary came to him in a dream last night and told him that you weren't in pain anymore. I'm not sure if he believes it was real. I do. Aunt Cindy, Tonto and I could swear we saw angels take you to Heaven twenty-seven days ago. I wonder if you asked God to send a sign that you were with him. Becca keeps telling us that you went home to Heaven and that Jesus is taking care of you. She's pretty smart for a seven-year-old. I know that you would want us to celebrate today. In my heart I'm celebrating, but I don't think anyone else really wants to acknowledge Easter Sunday, so I'll keep it to myself.

Dad's ham was different, to say the least. He hadn't cooked one in a while, I guess, because not too long after it was in the oven we began to smell something awful like burning plastic. Well, it turned out to be burning plastic. We couldn't eat it with the package burnt into the outer layer, so it went in the garbage. Instead, we ate the small turkey that Tonto had prepared as a backup plan. He followed your recipe to a tee and it was perfect. I think you must have been there to help because Tonto always has been more of a Spam and eggs kind of guy.

I'm going to come see you tomorrow morning to talk with you for a while.

Thank you for everything. God, I hope you can hear me,

Dara

———— ✥ ————

Mumo,

Tonight, I was with my boyfriend Chris at the fireworks and thought about you the whole time. You must have seen Fourth of July fireworks just about every year of your life until now. This time you didn't miss much—they really weren't that good. The finale only lasted three or four minutes, and it was mostly starburst explosions, not the shooting fountains that we like.

I ventured into your bedroom a little while ago to tell you Happy Fourth, because now that you're gone I have no one to be excited with. Earlier today Chris and I went to a picnic at his house and spent my favorite holiday with a family that sees no need to be patriotic. They couldn't answer why they were having a picnic in honor of a holiday that they think is silly. Maybe I love the Fourth so much because you raised me to. Either way, thank you for that sense of pride.

I'm sure your view is spectacular up there. I hope you're having fun and have made some new friends.

Don't forget about us.

I love you always,

Dara

—⟨⟩⟨⟩⟨⟩—

Mumo,

We didn't use the dining room this Thanksgiving because one of your electronic hospital beds is swallowing the room. So for the first time without you, we went to Aunt Celeste and Uncle Paul's to eat.

The stuffing was terrible, Gram, just big chunks of white bread with olive oil and pepper. It was nothing at all like yours. Aunt Celeste tried to get Tonto's mind off you, but he just sat slouching at the head of the lace-covered table and stared down at the food as if it were something from outer space. I don't think I have ever seen him that sad. I felt uncomfortable for him. Everyone was staring, Gram, and you know Tonto. He hates when people stare.

When we first sat down at the table I cried a little because you weren't next to him. He cried while he made you a plate of dry-white-meat turkey, bread ball stuffing, and a heap of mashed potatoes with corn in the center like you like it. No yams, Gram, none at all, and all I wanted was yours, brown-sugar-candied with marshmallows.

Uncle DD didn't come. He's been really weird since you died, and he fights with Tonto a lot, mostly about politics and religion. I think they fight so they never have to acknowledge that they actually feel something toward each other. Uncle DD can be rough on him, like he's mad about how he was raised. We all know you guys did your best, Gram, and now, without you here, Tonto doesn't go near him. It is probably better that way.

Uncle Paul said the prayer this year, because Tonto wasn't up to it. I felt as if I were a guest at someone else's family. You would have hated the fact that everyone tip-toed around, Gram. They were all afraid to laugh. I think we're allowed to be happy. I mean, we all know where you are.

It didn't smell like Thanksgiving, either. Becca kept asking if you were eating turkey with Jesus this year. If you did, Gram, I really hope he let you cook.

I'll write again at Christmas.

Love you,

Dara

———————

Mumo,

Merry Christmas! I hope everything is going well up there. I can guarantee that it's better than here. The porcelain angel you left with Mom is still on top of the tree. I can't help but picture you with the real angels, probably baking all of them cakes or helping them iron wrinkles out of their wings.

We had to put the tree up a little early this year, because Tonto wanted to get it out of the way. Truthfully, it was no fun at all. We weren't used to putting it up a whole month before Christmas. I can't believe it was only a few years ago that you sat here with us in your wheelchair and told us where to hang the ornaments.

I have big news for you. Tonto told me a little while ago

193

that he has always hated Christmas. He didn't say why, just that it had something to do with his dad. He said you never knew, that he never told you. He pretended to like it all of these years for you and for us.

Do you remember all those times we sat by the tree at night listening to the Alabama *Country Christmas* record? Mom's lap took the place of yours this year as official resting place for my head. We cried when we listened to the song about the empty chair. We glanced to the back of the room and realized that Tonto had put your wheelchair just where it always was, facing the tree.

He's still having a hard time with all of this. The envelopes were signed "Love, Mumo and Tonto," but no one said anything to him because we didn't think he even noticed that he did it. We stayed home for the whole holiday because no one felt up to going to Aunt Celeste and Uncle Paul's house for dinner. We had planned to, but Mom just ended up making crock-pot-chicken and noodles with sweet corn, Stove Top stuffing made with chicken broth like yours, and a little bit of mashed potatoes from the box. She tried hard for everyone, but you and I both know that Mom was never much of a cook. Tont didn't eat because he said he didn't feel well. I don't think he was telling the truth.

Mikey was your only grandchild that bought you a gift this year. It was from the Santa's Workshop at his school, and he wanted to take it to your grave. The snow is too bad today to go, though. We all might go with him tomorrow. Be waiting for something special.

194

I'll write you a poem soon.
Miss you so much,

Dara

———⌈⌈8/8/8⌉⌉———

Mumo,

Today was my wedding day, and although I can't explain how, I know that you were there with all of us. I hope you approved of a woman performing the ceremony outside. I still worry about things like that. Even though you're not here anymore, I want you to be proud of me. After you died, I decided that Catholicism wasn't working for me—all the rituals and stuff—so I became non-denominational Christian. That's why our wedding was a little different than what you're used to.

Mom was a nervous wreck the whole week, just snapping at everyone and rolling her eyes with her arms perched up on her hips. Dad was crying when he walked me down the aisle, so was my Chris—well actually, I guess it's safe to say almost everyone was crying. When Dr. Christopher Hodge was announced as the brother of the bride, his face lit up, Gram. I am so proud of my big bro. Although it was terrible how sick you got, it was a huge part of his decision to pursue a career in medicine. See, you're still an inspiration to all of us.

Last night, I spent the night at your house with Mom, Tont, and Mel, so that my groom wouldn't see me on our wedding day before he was supposed to.

195

I had the dream again in which Tont, Mom, Dad, Mel, Dr. Chris, and I are all in Dad's 1987 blue Chevy van driving down a desert road in a frenzy. Suddenly Dad slams on the brakes and throws us into reverse, turns his head around with his mouth wide open, and says, "I just saw Mumo walking along the side of the road back there—she was walking, I swear it!" I can't talk in the dream, no one but Dad can, but I know you are dead, and I know I am scared. I'm sitting in the third-row seat with Mel when we pull up to you. Dad gets out, opens the side door, and there you are. We all want to say so much, but we still can't talk. Tonto starts crying as he did the day you died, silent and hard. His eyes get really big, he opens his mouth to speak, and he says, "Dorothy, oh my God, Dorothy, but—but you're..." Then you say, "Hi-ya. You guys passed me up—thanks for comin' back, though. Why are you all so surprised? This was in the Bible, wasn't it? Now, we don't have much time, only six months—and I have to tell you everything." The only words we can speak are "Thank you, God, we love her, we love her so much."

That's when I woke up. It was six in the morning on my wedding day, Gram, and that's when I knew you would be there with me.

Tont wore his fancy blue wool suit jacket with blue dress pants and a red tie—the same thing he wears to every wedding, funeral, christening, and wake. Tont and I did a special dance, sorta like the father-daughter dance. The DJ called it a Tonto-Bride dance. I thought it was funny. The song was

"My Wish" by the country band, Rascal Flatts. The whole time Tonto was worried that everyone was staring at him and thinking bad things, but I told him he was silly and to concentrate on me. I told him I loved him and he did the sign of the cross on my head and said he wanted to stop, but we were only about a minute into the song. I know he hates to dance and that he danced at all was a gift.

Dr. Chris stepped in and finished out the song. Can you believe he had the nerve to tell me I couldn't dance? He started spinning me, dipping me, and moving me around like he actually knew what he was doing. I love my brother, Gram, and I love the way you and Tont raised us.

I don't know if you stuck around for the whole reception, but we did a special song for you. It was another country song, "When I Get Where I'm Going" by Brad Paisley and Dolly Parton. I lost it, Gram, I just broke down, but then I noticed that everyone was crying whether they were dancing or not. That's when I felt God there with us.

Two years and five months after you died, we still think about you, miss you, and love you more than ever. I want you to be here when Chris and I start a family and when I cook my first Thanksgiving turkey in our home. When the clouds won't leave, I want to see you fighting through them to show me the sun. I know you will, Gram. I pray I see you in my children's eyes and that I still make you as proud as I did before. And when it comes to my marriage, Gram, I hope you put a good word in for us with the Big Guy, because Chris and I have so much love to give one another—a love that is fashioned from God, you and Tont, Mom and Dad, and Chris' parents and grandparents.

I hope to write again soon. Thank you for helping me continue to grow in this life, this love, and this undying belief in something other than what I see.

Hope you enjoyed yourself today. I sure did.

I love you,

Dara

Au Revoir May

Jane Shortall

walked into the room in the retirement home to find May sitting upright in a high-backed chair. It was entirely in character that she wore a purple hat.

I live in France now and had flown back to spend an afternoon at May's new residence, high on a hill, overlooking the sea on the east coast of Ireland.

May was a true dame, old and frail now, yet unchanged in so many ways. She had a radiant, youthful air and plenty of the old brio about her.

She was smiling broadly, her arms outstretched in welcome, the same look in her eyes that I had seen and loved all my life. Madly pleased to see her, I rushed over and gave her an enormous hug. She felt thin—very, very thin. Her kind face was more lined and she was much weaker than the last time I had seen her. She gave me one of her big smiles.

It is a moment I will treasure forever. She died so soon afterwards.

—⟨⟩⟨⟩⟨⟩—

As a young woman, May was tall, with masses of beautiful dark hair. She wore tailored suits and red lipstick, and had quite a collection of shoes. Old photos place her firmly in the Dorothy Lamour camp of good-lookers. When I was in my early teens I loved gazing at those stylish black-and-white photographs of May and her sisters.

Children of an artist father, they grew up beside the sea, in a wonderful world of color. Even in later years, they seemed exotic creatures. In the Ireland of the time they definitely would have turned heads.

And May most certainly did. My grandfather's head was one of them.

They met in the early fifties, a long time after his first wife, my grandmother, had died when still a young woman. In no time he married May and went on to enjoy years of happiness and another daughter, a stepsister for my mother.

As a result of this happy encounter, May was part of my life from the day I was born.

—⟨⟩⟨⟩⟨⟩—

In the weeks before my trip back to Ireland, the news about her health was not good. A stroke had affected her eyesight and she could only see shadows and strong colors.

I fussed about a gift. What was the use of something May couldn't see, perhaps upsetting her?

200

Then, I found just the thing, a richly colored, vintage, long, thick, crushed velvet scarf. With half a foot of shiny pearls sewn into each end, it was no gift for a mousy female. This made it just right for May.

After we had afternoon tea in the excellent place she had moved to live, I produced my present to shrieks of delight. May felt the soft velvet material, then the pearls at each end. "It's me," she said. "Perfect!"

She held it up to her face, wrapped it around her neck, and informed a nurse who popped in, "Look, this is from my granddaughter. Here she is. She's come all the way from France to see me and brought me this beautiful scarf from Paris. Isn't it wonderful?"

Later, as we went on a tour of the nursing home, she announced to everyone we met, "Hello, this is my granddaughter, isn't she lovely?"

And I (not in the first flush of youth) did feel lovely.

I wondered if I would cope as well with a similar situation: a small room, with what seemed like one percent of her possessions, needing help with almost everything, and yet with a dazzling smile.

Despite many health problems, she told me she was happy and peaceful, and felt safe. She enjoyed looking out over the sea or relaxing in her room, listening to her big band music of the thirties and forties, remembering other times.

Perhaps seeing someone we love with every fiber of our

being when they are old, when they simply cannot manage without constant care, makes us take stock. It makes us stop wasting time watching endless TV or pursuing other useless activities. It nudges us to knuckle down *now* to all those things we said we'd definitely do, but never seemed to get started on.

I left the home on the hill and spent a lot of time thinking about May and her long life and her substantial influence on me, especially as a young woman. My life today had become a little sluggish.

I returned to France and set about changing a few things. I rearranged a room so I now have a proper dressing room. I too have always been interested in fashion and have quite a collection of jewelry. Why not have things I love around me?

It is in this room, surrounded by things I treasure—a few pictures of May among them—that I write, beside the window looking out over the foothills of the Pyrenees.

I took a very old, small table, painted it blue and yellow, and covered it in fringed shawls. This is where my laptop sits. And I have a few new projects up and running. Two articles are awaiting publication with excellent journals, three more are ready to submit, and half a dozen are in the early stages. At least twice each week, I add a few hundred words to a bigger project, a book that has long been simmering in my head.

It's as if I have been given some sort of grace to do what I love more than anything else. I want to use the rest of my time to plan my projects, to take the path that is right for me, not to fritter away the rest of life.

I recently read something wonderful in a literary journal. The subject was aging. The piece had all the usual stuff, that sixty and seventy are nothing at all, and there are people who swim and dance into their nineties.

The best bit was that studies have shown that the people who go on to really enjoy and even thrive in their old age are women who write. And there's more: those who started late in life have marvelous futures, because they have so much to say. What a splendid thought is that?

―――⟨⟨⟨⟩⟩⟩――――

Knowing May helped me appreciate beautiful things and how priceless is a happy disposition.

Saying goodbye to May made me realize how precious are the years when we have the ability to go for it—to follow our dreams, wherever they lead. And we must...because time is too important to waste.

So, when the time comes and I must slow down a little and accept the changes that aging brings, I hope I'll be happy to sit at a little table, doing what I love best—maybe even wearing a purple hat.

Contributors

Multi-award winning author **Diana M. Amadeo** is proud to have five hundred publications with her byline in books, anthologies, magazines, newspapers and online. Yet she humbly, persistently, tweaks and rewrites her thousand or so rejections with eternal hope that they may yet see the light of day. She can be reached at home.comcast.net/~da.author/site/.

A writer of essays, feature stories, and poetry, **Ann Reisfeld Boutté**'s work has appeared in many publications. She has a Master's Degree in Journalism from American University and has worked as a feature writer for a daily newspaper and a national wire service. In 2009, she won third place in the Artists Embassy International's Dancing Poetry Contest and an honorable mention in the Texas Poetry Calendar awards. She was a Juried Poet in the Houston Poetry Fest in 2001, 2005, and 2009. You can contact her at AnnRBoutte@gmail.com.

Dianna Calareso is a writer, editor, and writing instructor. Since earning her MFA in Creative Writing from Lesley University, she has been published in various online and print journals, including *Concisely, paradigm, Wilderness House Literary Review,* and *Falling-Apart.net.* She recently completed her first memoir, *At Ease,* and continues to write nonfiction essays with a special interest in family memoir. She can be reached at dcalareso@hotmail.com, and her work can be found at dcalareso.blogspot.com. Dianna lives in Nashville, Tennessee, with her husband and two cats, Lucca and Bella.

Alison Cameron is half English, half French. Growing up, she traveled the world thanks to her diplomat dad and is happily settled in Southern California with her American husband and daughter. While earning a living as a kindergarten teacher and hotel concierge, she has both taken and taught innumerable writing classes. Writing has been her North Star. She has written three unpublished novels, starting with *The Mystery of the Grand Piano* when she was five years old. Follow Alison's blog, "Meditation: Cradling the Crying Child" (meditation-cradlingthecryingchild.blogspot.com/), which explores how meditation helps people cope with daily life.

Eva Maria Chapman has successfully pursued a variety of careers before launching into writing. Her first book, *Sasha and Olga,* a memoir (Lothian 2006), charts the adversities of her Russian refugee family, before and after emigrating to Australia. "Butterflies and Demons" unveils the extraordinary past of the Kaurna Adelaide Aborigines. "Russian Roulette 2020" (*Shine*, Solaris 2010) is a love story set in a future dominated by Internet live-streaming. She lives in a wildlife sanctuary on the edge of Exmoor, England, with husband Jake. When not writing, she likes to make hats, grow vegetables, and frolic with her grandchildren. Her website is evamariachapman.com.

Denise Emanuel Clemen's publications include the *Georgetown Review*, *Two Hawks Quarterly*, *Literary Mama*, and *The Mom Egg*. She's received fellowships to The Virginia Center for the Creative Arts, Vermont Studio Center, and Ragdale, and was an Auvillar fellow at *Moulin á Nef* in France in 2009. Denise has a completed memoir manuscript and a novel in progress. She is a blogaholic and blogs about three of her favorite topics—divorce, adoption from the birthmother point of view, and France—at hisbigfatindianwedding.blogspot. com, deniseemanuelclemen.blogspot.com and myfrenchunderpants.blogspot.com.

Kate Dernocoeur moved on from a twenty-five-year career as an emergency medical services journalist, earning her MFA (nonfiction) from Western Michigan University in 2010. Her first major literary publication was in *Fourth Genre* (Spring 2010). Home base for this Colorado native has been in Lowell, Michigan, for many years, so she yearns for any excuse to travel—particularly to remote natural settings. So far, she has found the time, resources and gumption to see more than thirty-five countries, traveling on foot, in rafts and kayaks, and on horseback. She is always ready for the next adventure.

Maria Duffy lives in Dublin, Ireland, with her husband and four young children. She embarked on her writing journey only three years ago and has enjoyed some success already. She's had poems published in an online fairy tale magazine and another story published in an Irish collection of short stories, *A Pint and a Haircut*. She's currently editing her first novel and working on her second. She writes two blogs—writenowmom.wordpress.com and lookingfor-laughs.wordpress.com. She's also recently started to blog for *Hello! Magazine*. Contact her at mariaduffy2@gmail.com and find her on Twitter at @mduffywriter.

Terri Elders, LCSW, lives near Colville, Washington, with two dogs and three cats. A public member of the Washington State Medical Commission, she received the 2006 UCLA Alumni Community Service Award for her work with Peace Corps. Her stories and articles have appeared in over thirty anthologies and dozens of periodicals. She blogs at atouchof-tarragon.blogspot.com, and can be friended on Facebook or contacted at telders@hotmail.com.

The day **Mary Ellington** discovered more pens than lipstick in her purse she knew her fate as a writer was sealed. A member of Chat Noir Writers Circle, Mary has been published in the Florida State College at Jacksonville newspaper, *The Campus Voice*, as well as care-givers.com. Mary is currently blogging about her life as a caregiver for her ninety-three-year-old father. You can visit her at mellington.blogspot.com.

Betty Jo Goddard has traveled a packed road, acquiring a BS, an MA, and twenty-five years of teaching's bruises, successes, smiles, and love. She retired from teaching in 1983 and now lives with her three errant huskies in a solar-powered home on a ridge top in Alaska. After retiring from teaching, Betty Jo took up writing as a hobby. She has published two books and is working on a third. Her stories have appeared in *Dog and Kennel*, *Grit*, a *Cup of Comfort* anthology, and other publications both on and off line. Find her website at freewebs.com/bettyjogoddard.

Deanna Hershiser's essays have appeared in *Runner's World*, *BackHome Magazine*, *Relief Journal*, and other places. She lives with her husband in Oregon and blogs at deannahershiser.com/stories-glimmer.

Dara Hodge-LaRue is a 2009 graduate of Carlow University's MFA in Creative Writing program with a concentration in Creative Nonfiction. Her manuscript entitled *Holding My Breath*—from which "The Mumo Letters" is drawn—is a collection of essays chronicling her experiences as an awkward child growing up as part of an Italian-American family in the depressed town of Braddock, Pennsylvania. She also writes prose poetry regularly and her poems have been published in various publications. Dara wishes to thank her family, colleagues, and mentors for their support in the writing of this manuscript. She can be reached at daralarue@gmail.com.

Katrin Horowitz published her first novel, *Power Failures*, in 2007. She lives in Victoria, British Columbia, where she was one of the winners in a 2009 prose competition. In 2010 several of her shorter works were included in *Pathways Not Posted*, an anthology of poetry and prose. She is currently finalizing a new novel and working on a series of shorter pieces.

Ann Ingalls has been published in numerous publications, including *The Kansas City Star, Highlights, Highlights High Five, Way of St. Francis, Babytalk Magazine, Primary Treasure, Reiman Publications, Adams Media* and *Learning Express LLC.* Ann is currently promoting *Little Piano Girl*, a picture book about Mary Lou Williams, the first lady of jazz. Ann lives in Kansas City with her husband. You may contact her at anningallswrites.com.

Roberta Beach Jacobson, from Lake in the Hills, Illinois, makes her home on a far-flung Greek island. She has ghosted, coauthored, edited, translated, fact-checked, or contributed to dozens of nonfiction books published on four continents. You can find out more at RobertaBeachJacobson.com.

Gail Kirkpatrick writes about people and places that inspire us to keep doing what we do best. In her freelance work, she has written about programs for the homeless, plans for greener cities, innovative researchers, dedicated artists, and young entrepreneurs. Her creative nonfiction and fiction also explore history and connections with nature. This fall she will become a Masters candidate in the English and Creative Writing Department at Lancaster University. Gail lives in British Columbia, Canada, and recollects her rambles in and around, over and through Mt. Douglas Park at gailkirk-patrick.wordpress.com.

Kathe Kokolias is a writer living in Colonie, New York, and Ixtapa, Mexico. She has read her essays on National Public Radio and her writing has been published online as well as in a variety of newspapers, magazines, and anthologies including Travelers' Tales' *A Woman's World Again,* a collection of women's travel stories. Kathe has published a collection of essays entitled *Spandex & Black Boots: essays from an abundant life,* and her travel memoir of Mexico, *What Time Do the Crocodiles Come Out?* will be released in November 2010. You can contact her at kathekokolias@aol.com or visit her website at kathekokolias.com.

A freelance magazine writer, **Jennifer Lang** has been published in *Parenting, American Baby, Real Simple, Yoga Journal, Parents, Woman's Day* and *Natural Solutions,* among others. Her essays have appeared in the *South Loop Review, San Francisco Chronicle* and on *Ducts.org, the webzine of personal stories.* Visit her website at yogaprose.com.

An award-winning author and professional storyteller, **Molly Lemmons** has been published in numerous periodicals as well as newspapers in Arkansas, Texas, and Oklahoma. She retired from Mustang Public Schools to pursue writing and storytelling. She teaches classes on writing memories from the heart and is an alumna of Oklahoma Christian University. She lives in Mustang, Oklahoma, with her husband of fifty-three years and her three cats and a dog. You can reach her at mollyloubelle@cox.net and view her website at mollyloubelle.com.

Maryann McCullough is a retired math teacher from Phoenix, Arizona. A new writer of memoir and personal essays, she recently learned that her maiden name (Shanahan) comes from the Gaelic for storyteller, and feels that, at sixty-seven, she has found her true calling! She has been published in print and online magazines, among them *Quiet Mountain Essays*, *U.S. Catholic*, and *Monsoon Voices*. You can contact her at msm100@cox.net or read more of her writing at maryannmccullough.wordpress.com.

Mary E. McIntyre is a member of Life Writers Ink and The Writers Community of Durham Region. Her story "Scugog at Dark" won the short story contest for a Unionville Memoir Writers Alzheimer's Fundraiser. Her article "30,000 Reasons to Cruise Georgina Bay" appeared in the Parry Sound newspaper, *The Beacon*, while her poem, "Ugly Like a Scar" is included in the Poetry Module of Pearson Educational Publishing's textbook, *Live Lines*. In her forthcoming book, *Washburn Island: A Memoir of Childhood*, a violent tragedy tests the strong ties of a British immigrant family at Lake Scugog's Washburn Island, where generations of her family summered for nearly sixty years. See Mary's blog at maryemcintyre.wordpress.com.

Amy Munnell has been a freelance writer for nearly twenty-five years. Her work has appeared in various publications including the *Chocolate for a Woman's Soul* series, *From the Heart: Vol.*

2—More Stories of Love and Friendship, *Points North*, *ByLine*, *Athens Magazine* and *Georgia Magazine*. She and her writing partner have taught workshops and classes on writing nonfiction and currently have a nonfiction book proposal circulating with an agent and a children's book in the planning stage. Amy is on the Board of Directors of the Southeastern Writers Association and serves as its co-president.

Stephen Parrish is the author of *The Tavernier Stones*, published in May 2010 by Midnight Ink. He is a graduate of the University of Louisville and the University of Illinois, and presently lives in Germany where he is at work on his next novel. You can reach him at steve@stephenparrish.com.

Robert B. Robeson has had more than 725 articles, short stories, and poems published in over 250 different publications which include *Reader's Digest*, *Positive Living*, *Official Karate*, *Vietnam Combat*, *Frontier Airline Magazine*, and *Newsday*, among others. He's also been featured in seven books and anthologies and has won four national Amy Writing Awards. His articles and short stories have gained a readership of millions in 130 countries. Robeson is a professional (life) member of the National Writers Association, the Distinguished Flying Cross Society, and the Military Writers Society of America. He's also a former newspaper managing editor and columnist.

Glynis Scrivens has been writing stories for women's magazines for the past nine years. She has had stories published in Australia, the United Kingdom, the United States, Ireland,

Sweden, Norway, Denmark, South Africa and India. She has won prizes in competitions. She also interviews and writes nonfiction articles for magazines such as *Writers' Forum* and *Ireland's Own,* and has essays in several U.S. anthologies (*Good Dogs Doing Good* and *Women Reinvented*). Glynis lives in Brisbane, Australia, with her husband and children—plus a dog, a cat, a rainbow lorikeet, guinea pigs, hens, and a young rat called Norbert.

Ruth Schiffmann spent fourteen rewarding years home-schooling her two daughters. As they got older she found herself with more time to write. Caring for her parents throughout her mother's struggle with depression and her father's decline with dementia has inspired much of her work. More than a hundred of Ruth's stories and articles for children, teens, and adults have appeared both online and in print. To read more of her work, visit RuthSchiffmann.com.

Jane Shortall's writing has appeared in numerous publications, including *The Irish Times, Independent, Medical Times, Evening Herald, Kilkenny People, Meath Chronicle, La Depeche du Midi,* and in glossy magazines *France Magazine, French Property News, Irish Country Sports and Country Life,* and *Ireland's Horse.* She has been featured on Irish Radio and is a regular writer for seniorwomen.com in the United States. Jane, who was born in Ireland, lives with her husband in a remote part of southern France, close to the Pyrenees. She is working on a novel. She can be contacted at jane-shortall@hotmail.com.

Annmarie B. Tait resides in Conshohocken, Pennsylvania, with her husband Joe Beck and Sammy the "Wonder Yorkie." In addition to writing stories about her large Irish Catholic family and the memories they made, Annmarie also has a passion for cooking, sewing, and crocheting along with singing and recording Irish and American folk songs. Annmarie has had more than twenty stories published in various anthologies, including *Chicken Soup for the Soul, Patchwork Path,* the HCI *Ultimate* series and *Reminisce Magazine.* You may contact Annmarie at irishbloom@aol.com.

A bilingual freelance journalist and feature writer, **Iwona Tokc-Wilde** lives on the south coast of England. "The Sea Monster" is her first short story. Iwona has an eclectic background: a Masters in English Literature and Literary Theory, a teacher of English as a Second Language, and a career development coach. She is also a qualified accountant but words, not numbers, are her first love. Iwona writes for serious UK and Polish magazines and tries to be funny at thelaughingwife.blogspot.com. You can contact Iwona at iwonatw@yahoo.co.uk.

Susan Weich is a columnist with the *St. Louis Post-Dispatch* and currently is an MFA student at Lindenwood University. She lives in St. Charles, Missouri, with her husband Dean, son DJ, daughter Rachel, and four pets—dogs Oshie and Skittles, a cat named Biscuit, and Bill the box turtle. You may contact her at sweich7@gmail.com.

Reading Group Guide

1. What is your reaction to this collection of stories as a whole? Did you have any unexpected feelings or responses? Did it bother you that humorous stories were mixed in with serious stories?

2. Of the stories that dealt with death or dying, which one(s) had the most impact on you? Why?

3. Of the stories that dealt with other aspects of saying goodbye, which one(s) were most memorable to you? Why?

4. Have you had any personal experiences with caregiving? How do your personal experiences compare to the experiences of people in these stories?

5. Think of a time when a friend of yours experienced loss, such as a death in the family, the death of a pet, a divorce, or a job loss. What did you do or say to help that

person? Was it difficult for you to find the right thing to do or say?

6. How do you give support and comfort to a person who doesn't want support or comfort?

7. What was your first experience with death or dying? What lessons did you learn? Did your experience change your views about living and dying?

8. What does the expression "dying well" mean to you? What would be a "good death" for you when that time comes?

9. In "The Evolution of Your Goodbyes" by Ruth Schiffmann, the author describes what it's like to watch as a parent loses memory. Do you know someone with Alzheimer's disease, dementia, or other diseases that cause memory loss? How did your experience compare to the author's?

10. In "Love Letters" by Mary E. McIntyre, the author wants to read old letters her parents wrote to each other, but her father keeps his vow to destroy them after his wife's death. Did the father make the right decision? Why or why not?

11. "Holding Him Softly" by Denise Emanuel Clemen and "Dreaming as the Summers Die" by Terri Elders are both stories of adoption. In what ways are these stories similar? In what ways are they different? How do these stories compare to any personal experiences you have had with adoption?

12. In "Finding the Words" by Maria Duffy, the author is concerned about how her young children will react at

their grandfather's funeral. What were your experiences as a child at funerals? How would you handle it if you had to escort a young child to a funeral today?

13. In "Ghosthouse" by Roberta Beach Jacobson, the author makes a trip to revisit her childhood home, only to find that it is gone. Have you ever visited your childhood home? How did the experience match your expectations?

14. "Turning in My Keys" by Ann Ingalls is a story about retirement. Are you retired, or do you know somebody who has retired recently? What was the last day of work like?

15. "Puppy Love" by Susan Weich tells the story of a death of a pet. Have you ever experienced the death of a pet? How is the death of a pet similar to and different from the death of a person?

16. In "A Bloody Good Party" by Alison Cameron, the author's father takes an active role in planning his funeral arrangements. Have you discussed your final wishes with those who are close to you? Why or why not?

17. Have you had the experience of being able to reconcile with someone before they died? What was that like for you and how did you know the time was right to do so?

18. What role does storytelling play when it comes to death, dying, and other aspects of saying goodbye? Does it make a difference to the dying person to know they will be remembered in stories? Does it make a difference to survivors to be able to remember a person in stories?

About Dream of Things

Dream of Things publishes memoirs, anthologies of creative nonfiction, and other books. We seek memorable stories and distinctive voices. Submission guidelines and payment information can be found on the Dream of Things website.

We are currently accepting creative nonfiction stories for anthologies on a variety of topics, including forgiveness, Internet dating, travel, coffee shops, and life in the modern workplace. For a complete list of current anthology topics, visit the Dream of Things Workshop at dreamofthings.com.

OTHER BOOKS FROM DREAM OF THINGS

Everything I Never Wanted to Be
A memoir of alcoholism and addiction, faith and family, hope and humor by Dina Kucera
The true story of one family's battles with alcoholism and drug addiction over four generations, as told from the unique perspective of a grocery store clerk with a ninth-grade education who is trying to make it as a stand-up comic. A book that can change behavior and save lives—and make you laugh along the way.

MFA in a Box
A Why to Write Book by John Rember
By exploring the relationship between the writer and love, grief, place, family, race, and violence, John Rember helps you see how to go deep in your writing. He also tells you what you'll find there and how to get back. Along the way, you'll learn how to see the world as a writer sees it.

The Note
A book about the power of appreciation by Mike O'Mary
The powerful and ultimately uplifting message of *The Note* is that a simple note of appreciation can change a person's life and create positive feelings that ripple outward and touch an ever-expanding circle of people—including all who read this book.

Wise Men and Other Stories
A collection of holiday-related stories by Mike O'Mary
According to author Stephen Parrish, "O'Mary has a gift for simple, frank exposition of life's most poignant moments." In *Wise Men and Other Stories*, O'Mary shares that gift with all of us. Enjoy this priceless collection of humorous and thoughtful stories this season and for many holiday seasons to come.